The Humanism of the Bible

A SERIES OF VOLUMES

EDITED BY

Professor JOHN E. McFADYEN, B.A. (Oxon.), D.D.
(United Free Church College, Glasgow)

AND

Rev. D. RUSSELL SCOTT, M.A.
(Late Pusey and Ellerton Hebrew Scholar in the University of Oxford)

THERE are multitudes interested in literature and religion to whom nevertheless the Bible seems a remote and unattractive book—ancient and theological rather than modern and human. The aim of this series is to set forth the human experience that underlies and is reflected in the Bible. For, if the Bible commend itself to us in the end as, in some real sense, the Word of God, it comes to us, in the beginning, no less surely as the Word of Man, or words of men—words which throb with human emotion, and enshrine the greatest interpretation of human life.

The patient and brilliant researches of modern Semitic and classical scholarship have recovered the historical background of the Bible. This series is an attempt to recover its humanity, or rather its men—to help the readers of the Bible to feel that its writers were bone of our bone, and flesh of our flesh, men who knew perplexity and sorrow, and were well acquainted with our doubts and fears and grief. This is perhaps the aspect of the Bible that has been most neglected, and the aspect, too, which might be expected to appeal most powerfully to the average modern mind.

The volumes of the series do not propose to subject the Biblical books with which they deal to detailed exegetical comment—that has often been done before : rather will they seek, in a broad way, to interpret their spirit, and to indicate their permanent human interest and worth.

The following volumes have been arranged for :—

PESSIMISM AND LOVE—a Study in Ecclesiastes and The Song of Songs. By Rev. D. Russell Scott, M.A., Montrose.

THE INDIVIDUALITY OF PAUL. By Rev. R. H. Strachan, M.A. (Aberd.), B.A. (Cantab.), Minister of St. Columba's Presbyterian Church, Cambridge.

THE PROBLEM OF PAIN—a Study in the Book of Job. By Professor John E. McFadyen, D.D., Glasgow.

LIFE AND WORSHIP IN THE PSALTER. By Rev. Professor W. G. Jordan, D.D., Queen's University, Kingston, Ont., Canada.

STUDIES IN LIFE FROM JEWISH PROVERBS. By Rev. W. A. L. Elmslie, M.A., Fellow of Christ's College, Cambridge.

JESUS AND LIFE. By Rev. Professor Joseph F. McFadyen, M.A., Hislop College, Nagpur, India.

PESSIMISM AND LOVE

PESSIMISM AND LOVE

IN ECCLESIASTES AND
THE SONG OF SONGS

WITH TRANSLATIONS FROM THE SAME

BY

DAVID RUSSELL SCOTT, M.A.
MONTROSE;

LATE PUSEY AND ELLERTON HEBREW SCHOLAR
IN THE UNIVERSITY OF OXFORD

WIPF & STOCK · Eugene, Oregon

Wipf and Stock Publishers
199 W 8th Ave, Suite 3
Eugene, OR 97401

Apocalyptic Problems
By Hill, H. Erskine
Softcover ISBN-13: 978-1-7252-9107-2
Hardcover ISBN-13: 978-1-7252-9106-5
eBook ISBN-13: 978-1-7252-9108-9
Publication date 11/2/2020
Previously published by Hodder and Stoughton, 1916

This edition is a scanned facsimile of
the original edition published in 1916.

PREFACE

THIS preface is only necessary for the opportunity which it gives of making acknowledgments.

I am indebted for one or two illustrations in the earlier chapters of the book to the Expositions of Ecclesiastes by the late Rev. Samuel Cox, D.D.; and doubtless, throughout the book, to many other sources both for illustrations and ideas, for originality is scarce, and a striving after it but " vanity and vexation of spirit."

I have to thank the Rev. James Hastings, D.D., of Aberdeen, for his kindness in allowing the article on " The Wise Man " to be reprinted from *The Expository Times*.

Some of the studies made their first appearance clothed for the pulpit, and, no doubt, still wear, as they go to the press, part of their original dress. To those who suffered them in their sermonic form I feel that I ought to express my thanks, and, to any and all who may suffer them as they now are, my humble wish that the labour of reading will not be either a sore " weariness to the flesh " or a continuous " pursuit after wind."

D. R. S.

MONTROSE,
August, 1915.

CONTENTS

Introduction

	PAGE
Ecclesiastes = Koheleth	11

I. The Pessimist

The Cry of the Wearied Heart (Eccles. I. 1—11)	17
The Experiment with Wisdom (Eccles. I. 12—18)	28
The Experiment with Pleasure (Eccles. II. 1—11)	38
The Divine Programme (Eccles. III. 1—10)	49
Man and Beast (Eccles. III. 16, 18—21)	57
The Bed-Rock of Pessimism (Eccles. IV. 1—3; VII. 1*b*)	66
The Pessimist on Money: Three Cartoons (Eccles. IV. 4, 6—8; V. 10, 11, 13—17; VI. 1—6)	76
The Uses of Adversity (Eccles. VII. 2—4)	85
The Pessimist on Woman (Eccles. VII. 26—28)	93
Is God Neutral? (Eccles. IX. 2, 3)	101
The Words of the Pessimist	110

II. The Hedonist

Epicurus in the Old Testament	125

Contents

III. THE PIETIST

	PAGE
Good and Evil in the Pietist	139
The Gift of Life (ECCLES. II. 24*b*, 25; III. 13)	151

IV. THE SOPHIST OR WISE MAN

The Words of the Sophist	169
Two are Better than One (ECCLES. IV. 9—12)	175
Luck, or the Element of Chance in Life (ECCLES. IX. 11)	184
The Element of Risk in Life (ECCLES. X. 8, 9)	194
A Plea for Self-Cultivation (ECCLES. X. 10)	203
The Fable of the Charmer and the Snake (ECCLES. X. 11)	211
Imperfect Conditions (ECCLES. XI. 4)	222

LOVE SONGS OF THE BIBLE

Nuptial Songs	235
Fragments of Songs	253

INTRODUCTION

ECCLESIASTES = KOHELETH

Ecclesiastes is the translation in the Greek Bible called the Septuagint of a Hebrew word, *Koheleth*, whose meaning it is hopeless to fix with accuracy. All that we can say is that the word has something to do with a congregation or an assembly, hence the suggested translations, " a leader of an assembly," or " the assembly itself," " a debater," " a preacher," " a great orator." Of these translations, " an assembly " might seem to fit in best with the nature and contents of a book which is an assemblage of different conceptions of life and conduct. The final literary editor, whoever he was, of this book no doubt intended it to appear as a whole, and, perhaps, for this purpose, employed considerable editorial craftsmanship ; but his labours have created endless difficulties for later interpreters, who have been driven to desperate straits to reconcile the conflicting and contradictory views which the book, as a whole, presents. For the purposes of practical exposition and of arriving at an intelligent understanding of the contents of the book we lose nothing, I think it will be found, by neglecting the well-meant attempts at unification and regarding Koheleth as a small company or assemblage of the most divergent views on the meaning of life. All commentators have discovered different trains of thought in Koheleth :

Pessimism and Love

there is Pessimism, Hedonism, Deism, and Sophism (the exaltation of wisdom), and, for the most part, they have sought to explain those different modes of thinking as arising out of different moods or as the expression of a mental debate going on in the author's mind (like, *e.g.*, the poem " The Two Voices " of Tennyson). Koheleth, according to this manner of interpretation, is a man of moods or of conflicting opinions, but there is more than a difference of mood or even of contending opinion in the book : there is a difference in thought, in total outlook on life and the world. It is very difficult to think of one man as Pessimist, Hedonist, Deist, and Sophist and writing himself down in one book as such. The book presents us with distinct minds rather than with varying moods, and so Koheleth is a company in which Pessimist, Hedonist, Deist, and Sophist meet and declare their distinctive tenets and views on life and the world. A glance at the Table of Contents will show at once that this view is the frame on which the exposition in the following pages has been built ; the pages themselves will show the different parts assigned to the different minds ; and each mind made responsible only for its own part will show a mental consistency, which certainly does not belong to the book when viewed as a whole. In a word, in this book we have a consistent Pessimist, a consistent Hedonist, a consistent Deist, and a consistent Sophist.

The book may possibly be regarded as the work of one man in this sense :—that he gathered together different views of life and conduct, or the philosophies of different schools, and welded them together into their present form. But such work is rather that of an editor or compiler than that of a genuine author ; and,

Introduction

in any case, there would be still different and distinct minds in the book with different and distinct points of view. The Pessimist might, besides being the author of his own part, possibly have also acted the part of compiler ; but we cannot of course be certain, for we know practically nothing as to the means by which the book was brought into its present form.

After all, the first consideration is not how or by what means a book has attained to its final form, but rather, what the book actually contains in the way of illumination and truth, and Ecclesiastes, whatever critical views we may take of it, contains pessimism and hedonism, piety and wisdom.

NOTE.—In the Hebrew Bible " Koheleth " stands as the title of the whole book, but, in the book itself, Koheleth is a pseudonym for the Pessimist, except in Chap. XII. 9, where Koheleth is described as a Sophist. But Chap. XII. 9 is, no doubt, a note of some editor, who pays to Koheleth, the Pessimist, a compliment which he scarcely deserves. In the following expositions Koheleth is invariably the Pessimist.

I. THE PESSIMIST

I. THE PESSIMIST

THE CRY OF THE WEARIED HEART

The words of Koheleth, son of David, king in Jerusalem :—

Vanity of vanities, saith Koheleth ; vanity of vanities, the whole world is vanity.

What profit is there to man in all his toil with which he toils under the sun ?

One generation goes and another comes, while the earth remains standing for ever.

And the sun rises and the sun sets, going to its place and panting is it to rise there again.

Going into the south and circling into the north, circling, circling goes the wind and unto its circlings returns the wind ever again.

All the torrents go to the sea and the sea is not full ; unto the place where the torrents go, thither they go and go.

All things are full of a weariness which no man can declare ; and eye cannot be satisfied with seeing nor ear filled with hearing.

What has been will be, and what has been done that will be done, and there is no new thing under the sun.

Pessimism and Love

Is there a thing of which it is said " Lo, this indeed is new," already it hath existed in the ages which were before us.

There is no remembrance of our forbears nor will there be any remembrance of those who are yet to be, amongst those who come after them.—Chap. I. 1—11.

Vanity of vanities, all is vanity! With such hopeless words does this book open—words which, with little variance in form, have been often repeated and are still heard to-day, but which man, so long as he has retained a semblance of health and sanity, has never really believed ; if he had, he would have easily found some more or less agreeable means of ending his vain existence. The words in the interrogative form most common to-day—" Is Life worth living ? "— present a question which has been almost invariably and finally answered by the men who put the question living on and apparently being glad to do so in spite of the real or imaginary misery of their lot. To the selfish and whining pessimist, to the man who has a grudge against his treatment by the world, to any one tired and sick of life, no more wholesome tonic can be given than the one which Epictetus administered to such of his contemporaries as affected world-sickness. He told them that there were many exits from the theatre of life, and if they did not like the show they could retire by the nearest door and make room for men of a more modest and grateful spirit. No nervous anxiety need be felt in administering this tonic. It will have no fatal results. Even if it should do no

The Cry of the Wearied Heart

good, it will prove absolutely harmless in the case of whining complainers, morbid egotists, and selfish critics of life. But while this tonic may be the only possible and safe cure in the case of those who enjoy life by crying out against its vanity and by putting, with a deluded seriousness, the question, Is Life worth living ? it is not the treatment we are justified in meting out to Koheleth. He was not an immature youth ; he was a man of observation and experience, who courageously faced the facts of life and compels us to do the same, and, though his conclusions may be hopeless and even bitter, they left him with at least the one redeeming feature of a true compassion. Justice at least demands that we look at the facts which he saw and as he saw them and weigh the considerations which brought him to his hopeless judgment and reasoned conviction of the vanity of existence. Koheleth is no dainty *dilettante* playing idly with the facts of life. He thinks and he feels seriously and intensely ; he deserves sympathetic consideration, even though we, likewise thinking seriously and feeling intensely, are compelled to reject absolutely his hopeless words.

In this paragraph, full of the weariness of life and sighing with the weight of its mysterious burden, Koheleth advances certain facts and considerations which seem to prove the vanity of existence.

(i) There is the uselessness of all human labour. " What profit," he asks, " has a man of all his toil in which he toils under the sun ? " All human activity is in vain. Now to this hopeless conception of man's toil certain obvious answers can be at once given. By his labour a man can gain a competence, perhaps great

Pessimism and Love

wealth, and open for himself the gates which the key of gold unlocks. Let us suppose that by his labour this profit comes to a man. He gains a substantial competence; he becomes rich; the things that yield to money, comfort, refined luxury, possessions, the possibility of satisfying almost any personal desire, are in his power; he is a man of substance and has all the importance of such. Has he, however, by this increase made any real advance? Has he gained any real profit? It is a simple moral commonplace, which all men confess with their lips at least, that money is no guarantee of happiness and that increase of wealth does not mean increase of the joy of life. Koheleth knows that well, and, later in the book, we shall see the truth dramatically and powerfully depicted. In the pursuit of wealth a man has probably to deny himself many of the simple pleasures and innocent enjoyments of life; he has to " shun delights and live laborious days," and when the goal is attained he will look back and wonder whether the result has been worth all the self-denial; he has gained his end, but he has lost much on the way. How many rich men regard with envy the days of their comparative poverty and would fain charm back into life the peace and gladness of earlier times! No doubt this feeling is in part due to idealising, to the common tendency to tint the past, and the future as well, with the rose, and to keep our sombre colours for the present, but the fact remains, the present, even with its wealth, retains its sombre hue. Money provides food and raiment; it may clothe a man in purple and fine linen; it may carry on "the business" economically, generously or even extravagantly; it provides for the working expenses of life,

The Cry of the Wearied Heart

and as riches increase these have a way of increasing too; but profit is something over and above the working expenses, it is the gain which remains when all these have been fully met, and the question what profit is there in wealth to a man from all his toil with which he toils under the sun still remains a question. There is one satisfaction which money seems to bring to men in the sense of power. Men with money have power, and they feel their power and win a certain kind of happiness out of the feeling. But if the ideal of manhood is to be amongst men as one that serveth, and he that will be greatest among men shall be least of all, this sense of power is only a barrier between a man and his ideal, and the money which creates it becomes a positive evil. What profit is there, then, in money for all the toil in which a man toils beneath the sun?

But a man by his labour may win a reputation. But what is a reputation? It is a vapour, a mist, a brief and transitory thing at the best. Should it even last beyond a man's mortal years, should it place a man amongst the immortals of the earth, the man himself will leave his reputation behind, and who knows whether he will then have any profit or pleasure in it? A reputation is a pleasing satisfaction, brief and precarious; when it is lasting, it comes too late for mortal to enjoy; only to a great and self-deluding conceit can it prove a substantial reward and a real profit for a man's labour under the sun. Or a man by his work may bring blessing to others; he may increase the happiness in the world and bring comfort and gladness and freedom to men. The thought has inspired many a brave and faithful worker; but there is a fly in the ointment, for his work may never bring the blessing he

Pessimism and Love

hopes to see : those for whom he works may reckon little of the blessing ; they may even refuse it, or simply take it with greedy hands and in their hearts have no thought of the toil and sacrifice by which it has come. Social reformers know the bitterness of disappointment.

What profit is there in money, in reputation, in philanthropy for all the toil in which a man toils under the sun ? The question still remains a question.

(ii) Further, the processes of Nature and the brevity of man's life support the pessimistic conclusion of the vanity of existence. Nature presents us with processes which seem like ever-repeating cycles and endless repetitions. The sun rises and sets ; the process goes on day in and day out, apparently endless. It is the same with the rivers ; they flow and flow again to the sea, and yet the sea is not full. We may say it is the same with man : one generation cometh and another goeth, an endless coming and going of human life ; though, with regard to man, the thought of Koheleth is rather of the brevity of man's life—the brevity of an individual life and a single generation as compared with the apparent abidingness of Nature. *Natura est longa, brevis vita hominum.*

Nature repeats herself in endless cycles, and there is no new thing under the sun. The mighty wheels revolve unceasing, but they lead nowhere. Perhaps it may be said, Nature to us in these days presents, not an endless series of cycles, but rather a progressive movement, that there is an ascent or growth in Nature, and that evolution is a word of hope and prophecy, not of despair. But to immediate observation the world still appears very much what it was to Koheleth ; the

The Cry of the Wearied Heart

same features occur and re-occur with an endless monotony, day and night, summer and winter, sowing and harvest, the ebb and flow of waters; Nature clings tenaciously to her well-known paths. In a scientific and inventive age like ours no doubt it seems ridiculous to say that there is no new thing under the sun. There are wireless telegraphy, aeroplanes, national insurance, new theologies and new religions, new fashions in literature, art, and science; the very latest is always appearing, but how soon all such new things lose their freshness and their wonder and become the commonplaces of life. And we have to remember that all new inventions, wonderful as they are to us and beyond the most daring imagination of the past, are simply new combinations of forces and things that are as old as time itself, and they leave simply untouched the cardinal features of human life. Birth and death, work and rest, health and sickness, pain and pleasure, hope and fear, loss and gain, friendship, love, marriage, parenthood, bereavement, virtue, vice, temptation, remorse, all these are ours : they belonged to past generations ; they will belong to the generations unborn. As it was in the beginning, it is now and ever will be ; there is no new thing under the sun.

(iii) And further, in support of the truth of the vanity of existence, Koheleth reminds us of the truth that there is no remembrance of our forbears ; we too shall be forgotten, and our children and our children's children will receive the same fate. Not one in a thousand becomes immortal upon earth, and of his immortality it can be said " posthumous fame is but oblivion."

These are not exhilarating reflections ; they do not

Pessimism and Love

stimulate ; they do not set us on fire with enthusiasm for living. Well ; at the outset, it is advisable to remember that in the valuation of judgments upon life and of criticism of the world and human experience, one important consideration is the question—Who is the judge? And what manner of man is the critic ?—for in such judgments and criticism the personal element cannot fail to colour the critic's views. Who was Koheleth ? What kind of person was he ? What was the heart whose voice declared everything to be vanity and a pursuit after wind ? He was a Jew whose inherited faith had suffered shipwreck. He may have believed in God, but his belief was of a pale, thin, and cheerless order. He believed much more in a Nature with laws of iron necessity than in a living and personal God who doth wondrous things and new. He lived in an evil time, when life and property were insecure, when goodness and public service received little or no recognition, when social anomalies abounded, when corruption and espionage were rife, when all personal freedom was smothered by the weight of tyrannical power—in a time when national hope and aspiration were impossible. Then he was rich on a gorgeous and Oriental scale ; he never knew the necessity of working for a livelihood, and he lived by making experiments in living. He was a decadent living in a decadent age. His voice is that of a sick man crying out in impotent despair because he feels himself dying by inches in the midst of an order he cannot change and of a nature blooming insolently and for ever. His heart was diseased and can no longer drive the healthy blood through the veins and arteries of his life. His vision was impaired. His judgment was discoloured. Kohe-

The Cry of the Wearied Heart

leth has been called a voice crying in the wilderness of antiquity " Vanity of vanities ! All is vanity and a pursuit after wind "; but he is a voice that cries out of the city of modern civilisation, a voice that has perhaps vibrated in our own souls ; the voice of the wearied heart, of him whose vision is limited to things seen and temporal and who is without God and hope in the world ; the voice of sickness and not of health, whose words do not speak with complete and final authority on the meaning and purpose of life.

But perhaps the question may be asked why this voice of despondency, disappointment and defeat, of misery and scepticism, this voice of the decadent is allowed to utter itself in Holy Writ. As a matter of fact Koheleth did not get within the bounds of Scripture without difficulty. Jewish scholars debated his claim to a place in the Sacred College of Holy Writers. But they did elect him. And, whatever may have been the reasons for their decision, we cannot grudge him the honour nor complain that " in the great record of the spiritual history of the chosen and typical race, a place has been kept for the sigh of defeated hopes, for the gloom of the soul vanquished by the sense of the anomalies and mysteries of human life." True ; no Christian can subscribe to his faith, which is to him both incomplete and false ; but may not the presence of a faith, incomplete and even false, in the Scriptures be interpreted as a sign and symbol, as a kind of parable, that our imperfect faiths and mistaken beliefs are forgiven ? A sceptical creed did not keep Koheleth out of the Sacred Canon ; an imperfect faith will not keep a man out of the Kingdom. God pardons false and mistaken thinking as well as what we call our sins.

Pessimism and Love

The real value of Koheleth, however, lies in the fact that he just about hits the mark when he declares that life and the world are vanity. They are, when viewed apart from Christ and the light which comes from Him. Apart from Christ life is vanity and a pursuit after wind. Christ makes an infinite difference. He revolutionises all values. He turns the vanity into a glorious privilege. Christ, at the heart of God and in the world, means that love sits upon the throne of the universe, that love sustains and guides the world and has for the world a great and loving purpose. Let a man have that faith—a faith guaranteed in Christ and revealed by Him—he will not say that all is vanity and a pursuit after wind. His labour will not be in vain in the Lord. It will be part of love's gift to him, a communion in love, a means by which the great purpose of love is being worked out, a high privilege. His labour will be for the Eternal Kingdom of God. Should the Kingdom seem to tarry long and its complete realisation become vague and uncertain, he will, none the less, find through his work, his duty, and his daily discipline the Kingdom realising itself in his own heart and life. His work will bring to him profit, real profit, something that endures and is of true worth—patience, insight, obedience and peace. The man who works with faith in some great loving purpose of God works not in vain. And Nature, with its everlasting sameliness, will be changed. The brook may sing its unending song, as it slips and slides to join the brimming river, that men may come and men may go, while it goes on for ever; but its chatter, chatter, as it flows will be vocal with love and praise. How sweet and peaceful the murmuring brook is to the heart that rests in love.

The Cry of the Wearied Heart

And with Christ there will be at least one new thing. With Christ, God's redeeming love in his heart, inspiring it to a loving and redeeming service, the man himself will be a new creation. He will have a new vision of love streaming from an Eternal Sun, and transforming with its rays his own heart and the whole world of men and things. He will have the heart of love which is the heart of immortal youth, and youth ever finds the world a new place and full of new things.

Decadents, despondents, defeated and disappointed ones!—from Christ comes in exchange for your spirit of heaviness the garment of praise and the oil of joy for mourning.

" My soul, why art thou disquieted within me?
   Hope thou in God,
Who is the health of thy countenance
   And thy God."

THE EXPERIMENT WITH WISDOM

I Koheleth was king over Israel in Jerusalem.

And I gave my heart to search out and investigate by wisdom all that is done beneath the heavens : it is an evil business God hath given to the sons of men to be busied with.

I have seen all the works which are done beneath the sun ; and, behold, the whole is vanity and a striving after wind.

The crooked cannot be made straight ;
And what is lacking cannot be counted.

I spake with my heart saying, " As for me ! lo, I have become great and have increased wisdom, above all that were before me over Jerusalem, and my heart hath experienced in abundance wisdom and knowledge."

And I gave my heart to know wisdom, and to know madness and folly. I have known that this also is a striving after wind. For in much wisdom is much vexation, and he that increaseth knowledge increaseth pain.—CHAP. I. 12—18.

Koheleth has looked upon the activities of Nature and the life of man and has come to the pessimistic conclusion that all is vanity. Nature with her ever-

The Experiment with Wisdom

lasting sameliness and man with his profitless toil, both compel him to this melancholy judgment. But he does not at once accept this absolutely hopeless point of view. He will try through the instrumentality of wisdom to find some interpretation, some reasonable explanation of the facts as they have presented themselves. He will search out and investigate by wisdom all that is done beneath the heavens, with the hope, apparently, of finding some reasonable interpretation of man's life and Nature's ways. The intellectual experiment in which he purposes to engage is evidently a complex one, partly scientific and partly philosophic, that is, it consists in gathering together facts of human life, and then investigating them to discover their meaning. If we may use modern scientific terms, he is going to engage in anthropological and sociological research : he turns to the proper study of mankind which is man to see what wise meaning or purpose (if any) there may be in human life.

In the carrying out of this intention he has been pictured like the Arabian Caliph, the good Haroun Alraschid going forth in disguise to visit all quarters of the city ; to talk with barbers, druggists, calenders, porters, with merchants and mariners, husbandmen and tradesmen, mechanics and artisans ; to try conclusions with travellers and with the blunt wits of home-keeping men ; looking with his own eyes and learning for himself what their lives are like, how they conceive of the human lot, and what, if any, are the mysteries which sadden and perplex them ; trying to ascertain if *they* have any key that will unlock his perplexities, any wisdom that will solve his problems or help him to bear his burden with a more cheerful heart. In a word

Pessimism and Love

he was out for experience and its interpretation, to study man and society. We might imagine that this study of mankind, especially if it were carried out in the pleasant manner depicted, would be an agreeable occupation to a gentleman, like Koheleth, of position, leisure and abundant means. Research undertaken amidst the delights of travel, of seeing new faces and new scenes, of discovering new experiences, of being at perfect liberty to pursue one's own courses, has an enticing charm about it. But Koheleth, whatever method he pursued, found no charm and little delight in his investigations. He says that the work which God has given to the sons of men is an evil business, a woeful exercise, and he makes no exception of the work which he himself has voluntarily undertaken. He experienced no pleasure in it. He may have found after a time that his work became very monotonous ; that the people with whom he came into contact were, beneath certain external differences, all very much alike ; that human life in its experience of joy and sorrow, hope and fear, defeat and success, loss and gain, is very much one and the same the world over : and some people would certainly prove to be dull killjoys and personally objectionable, while the brightest and most agreeable only charm and interest for a season. Koheleth found his investigations in the human laboratory a sore trial.

And, further, not only was the method very irksome, the results of the investigation were disappointing in the extreme. He discovered that there were crooked things in the world that could not be made straight and deficiencies that could not be counted or made good.

The Experiment with Wisdom

" The crooked cannot be made straight ;
And what is lacking cannot be counted."

He is possibly here repeating a proverb which declares that there are evils and wants in life that cannot be remedied : they are inevitable and inexorable, so interwoven into the texture of human experience that the only way to remove them is by some effective cremation of the whole garment. He refers in later passages to certain moral and social anomalies which no doubt were amongst the inevitably crooked and deficient things. He says he knew princes who were fools ; servants who rode horseback while their masters (or who should be their masters) tramped on foot ; judges who sat on the seat of injustice ; good men who were despised and neglected ; bad men who were honoured. Any faint expectation he may have entertained, when he began his investigations, of finding a perfect moral and social world, or even finding one moderately good in its conditions, was woefully disappointed, and his disappointment was turned into despair as he felt the simple inevitableness and the unchangeableness of the evils in the world. The crooked, the deficient, the evil, all had to be. The only mending was the total ending of human existence.

From one point of view Koheleth was successful ; he applied his heart to gather knowledge and wisdom —he put energy and enthusiasm into his enterprise, and what he sought he gained, and could say, " Lo, I have become great and have increased wisdom above all that were before me over Jerusalem, and my heart hath seen in abundance wisdom and knowledge." This abundant knowledge, however, only the more

Pessimism and Love

revealed to him the evils of life and brought in its train an increase of disappointment and pain. His success was really his defeat. In gathering life he gathered sorrow. And further, his wisdom had not in itself any light or interpretation which might illumine the darkness; it could open no window or door to let in even a grey twilight which might presage a noontide coming veritably out of the blackness of night. Wisdom offered no philosophy, no solution, no interpretation of life. It is to this feeling of the intellectual bankruptcy of wisdom, in meeting the natural demand for some rational explanation of existence, that he most probably refers when he says that he gave his heart not only to wisdom, but to know madness and folly. He compared folly with wisdom, and found that the one had no advantage over the other. Before the inevitable and unchangeable evils of life, before, in fact, the widening orb of human existence, wisdom was as dumb as folly; in the interpretation of men and mankind the wise man became as the fool. The inevitable, the unchangeable, the mysterious, the evil, the crooked, and the defective thing pressed down and crowded in upon both, and both wise and foolish were equally helpless, with no light to give. Koheleth found no Divine philosophy that could give light and meaning to the world. Wisdom, as much as folly, is vanity and a pursuit after wind.

The experiment ended in disappointment and defeat; it only confirmed the feeling of deep pessimism. To this result the time in which Koheleth lived contributed in no small degree. It was an evil time; a time when genuine merit received little or no recognition, when there was no incentive to public spirit, when servility

The Experiment with Wisdom

and intrigue were the best policy, when there was little encouragement for the heroic and nobler impulses of man to express themselves, and when all the gracious charities and humane philanthropies of man had fallen asleep. It was not a time when enthusiasm, hope and brightness of outlook could easily and naturally flourish.

And with the same result no doubt the temperament of Koheleth had much to do. He was not, to say the least, a buoyant, hopeful and triumphant spirit, with power to will even in the darkest days a vision of brightness that would cause him to rejoice amidst tribulations (his own and other people's). It is easy to call him a natural pessimist or a decadent, and perhaps not altogether hard to justify the severity of the nomenclature ; easy to rule him out of court as a competent and fair-minded judge on life, till by regular exercise of the body and some tonic discipline of the mind he had got rid of his mental jaundice and become more capable of fair and wholesome judgment ; easy to scoff at his pessimistic conclusions as the unhealthy vagaries of temperamental weakness : but, making every allowance for the time in which he lived and for his temperament as factors contributing to his pessimism, it is almost certain that Koheleth, even though he had lived in other more hopeful days and been blessed with a more optimistic disposition, would have come to very much the same judgments upon human life. The really determining factor in his pessimism was not the time in which he lived, nor his temperament, but the mental presuppositions with which he started and the narrow limits within which his thought was confined. Koheleth in his methods was really a premature positivist, an antedated Comtist, a positivist

Pessimism and Love

philosopher born out of due time. Comte might have hesitated to claim him as a full-grown positivist, for there were in Koheleth still lingering traces of the child age, with its hold upon theology and its belief in God ; but these lingering rudiments of religion had so little practical effect on Koheleth's wisdom, experience, and life that he was as nearly a consistent positivist as human nature can be : certainly he was more consistent than the French philosopher. That is to say, Koheleth confined himself in his researches to *phenomena ;* he worked within the limits of the actual ; he had no light shining, as it were, out of the reason itself or out of the faith of the heart ; he had no eternal sun in whose light he could see light. His mind worked in a world of Nature, man and society, wholly contained within space and time. That world was his one reality. He was a positivist though born out of due time.

And no matter in what kind of age the positivist appears, and no matter what kind of temperament he possesses, if he is a consistent positivist—Comte was a most inconsistent one—he will come to a *cul-de-sac*, to a blank wall ; he will have facts, but no interpretation of them. For the world as confined within space and time has no final interpretation of itself ; it does not hold the key to the mystery of its own existence. However much we may know of the world (on positivist presuppositions), and however large our experience, it remains, as a whole and in itself, a dark mystery and induces with its darkness a feeling of vanity.

It would be unfair to say that all positivists and strict scientists—that is, scientists who should keep sternly to phenomena and do not superimpose on their

The Experiment with Wisdom

science or interweave in it any philosophical theory with implied transcendental ideas—are pessimists. Far from it. Many of them, scorning metaphysics and theology, are the boldest of optimists, speaking with boundless assurance of progress in Nature, man and society. But in speaking of progress they have ceased to be consistent positivists and strict scientists, for " progress " implies an end, a goal, something as yet phenomenally non-existent : the conception of progress contains a transcendental idea, the idea of a perfect consummation, of a final and triumphant completion of the world. And it is from some such transcendental idea, which is not a phenomenon and which lies really outside the region of the strict scientist and consistent positivist, that they really, though perhaps unconsciously, draw the boldness of their optimism.

John Fiske, the eminent American exponent of evolution, has in his " Destiny of Man " the following eloquent and optimistic words :—" Has all this work (of long evolution) been done for nothing ? Is it all ephemeral, all a bubble which bursts, a vision that fades ? On such a view the riddle of the universe becomes a riddle without a meaning. The more thoroughly we comprehend that process of evolution by which things have come to be what they are, the more we are likely to feel that to deny the everlasting persistence of the spiritual element in them is to rob the whole process of its meaning. It goes far toward putting us to permanent intellectual confusion, and I do not see that any one has yet alleged, or is ever likely to allege, a sufficient reason for accepting so dire an alternative. For my own part, therefore, I believe in the immortality of the soul, not in the sense in

Pessimism and Love

which I accept the demonstrable truths of science, but as a supreme act of faith in the reasonableness of God's work." There is no pessimism here, but a courageous optimism. There are the greatest of transcendental ideas, God and Immortality. There are theology and religion. The man of science is a man of faith, and from his faith he derives his hope and bold expectations. Take away all that is transcendental, all that is of faith and religion, confine him as Koheleth was confined, to phenomena alone, and he would be compelled to the judgment, "All is vanity and a striving after wind."

There is a wisdom that goes forth into the world of men and things, and gathers there much lore, but little light ; there is a wisdom that on the wing of faith rises to the heavens and beholds the Sun of Eternal Wisdom and Love, and in His Light sees Wisdom and Love and Light in all the world. That wisdom of faith does not make a man a shallow optimist saying all is well, even the crooked which cannot be made straight and the defective which cannot be made good. No ! evil is evil, but over evil, and working in it, Faith sees Wisdom and Love and Power. Faith sees God and believes that God will be equal to every demand an imperfect world makes upon Him—upon His power and love—on its way to perfection. A wise and loving God could not possibly make a world of men and things in which all is vanity and a striving after wind. He could only make a world with a purpose and an end such as Wisdom and Love would prescribe. To Christ the world was rich in meaning and purpose, and He saw it sanely and He saw it whole. To Him there was beauty in it, the beauty of the flowers in the meadow and birds on the

The Experiment with Wisdom

wing, of spring days when the farmer sows his seed, of suns setting in a sea of fire, of children playing in the market place; and much faith and goodness often in unexpected quarters: there were gracious women and true men in the world. But it was not all beauty and faith and goodness: there were crooked things—publicans growing rich by extortion, hypocrites mounting to Moses' seat, subtle, cruel foxes couched on thrones, scribes hiding the key of knowledge, and the blind multitude following their blind leaders into the ditch; there was disease and sin and death. In His world there was much to gladden and much to give sorrow and tears, but over all was the Eternal Father, loving and wise, the Creator taking full responsibility for His whole creation, the Redeemer who out of all evil could bring good. That faith made full the joy of the Man of Sorrows.

THE EXPERIMENT WITH PLEASURE

And I said in mine heart, " Come now : I will try thee with mirth and do thou try pleasure." And lo ! even this is vanity. Of laughter I said, " It is mad ! " And of mirth, " What doeth it ? "

I decided within me, to cheer my flesh with wine (yet I continued to behave myself wisely), and to lay hold of folly, until I should see where is this pleasure for the sons of men which they have beneath the heavens all their life long. I did great things. I built houses for myself ; I planted vineyards for myself. I laid out for myself gardens and parks and planted in them all kinds of fruit trees. I made pools of water for myself from which to water a wood with sprouting trees. I bought men-servants and maid-servants, and servants born in the house were mine ; yea cattle-steadings and sheep-runs were mine in abundance ; I had more than all that were before me in Jerusalem. I gathered for myself silver and gold and the choice treasures of the kings and the provinces. I got for myself men singers and women singers and the delights of the sons of men. . . . Yea, I became great

The Experiment with Pleasure

and increased above all that were before me in Jerusalem, yet my wisdom remained by my side. And all that mine eyes desired I withheld not from them, and I kept not my heart from any delight, for my heart was delighting in all my labour, and that was my portion from all my labour. And I turned to consider all my works which my hands had made, and to the labour which I had put forth in my work; and lo! the whole is vanity and a pursuit after wind, and there is no profit beneath the sun.

CHAP. II. 1—11.

Pessimism, in the abstract, may seem to have little to do with pleasure, but pessimists themselves, though they may vilify pleasure, regarding its value as negative (as only a release from pain), or delusive, or vastly outweighed by the sufferings of mortality, do not deny its actual existence, nor do they refuse for themselves the wine and honey of life. Koheleth is no less a pessimist because he makes rich trial of pleasure and good living; indeed, the trial only adds another vanity to life, confirming him in his despairing belief. After having made an ineffectual experiment to find the worth of wisdom and knowledge, he turns to pleasure very much in the same way as Goethe's Faust, who, having failed to solve life's problems by study, plunges deep in delights that he may thus " still the burning thirst of passionate desire."

"I said in mine heart, 'Come now: I will try thee with delights and do thou try pleasure'"; and his

Pessimism and Love

heart made most willing response. He was no laggard at the trial, nor slack in the carrying out of his purpose. He made great works; built houses; planted vineyards; laid out gardens and parks, where there were all kinds of fruit-trees; constructed ponds to irrigate the place where the young trees were reared. (Let it not be thought that all the hard manual labour involved in these undertakings was performed by Koheleth.) He bought men and women servants and had servants born in his house; his domestic comforts were not at all neglected. He possessed great flocks and herds, silver and gold in abundance, choice and royal treasures. He patronised the Muse, collecting for his delight both men and women singers. Everything that the eye could desire or the heart could wish was his. He went along a path luxuriant with pleasure and costly delights. Nor did he go like a fool diving madly into every excess, but his wisdom stood by him, making him discreet in this generous trial of sumptuous and good living. But alas for the result! It was all vanity and pursuit after wind. Of laughter he said, " It is mad! " Of delight, " What doeth it ? "

This experiment in pleasure was distinctly unhappy. It cost a great amount of money, thought, and labour, but yielded no satisfactory result. The whole business ended in disappointment and disgust, and was condemned as vanity and a pursuit after wind. I suppose most people feel that if they had Koheleth's opportunities, his vast wealth and property at their disposal, they could and would make a more satisfactory and satisfying business of life. They see, probably at once, where he failed. They may call his experiment a sinful extravagance, a reckless abandonment to

The Experiment with Pleasure

luxury, or a selling of the soul to pleasure, which can only lead to satiety and disgust. The man who so extravagantly gives himself to pleasure, if he do not come to sitting at table with the swine, will certainly come in the end to be without appetite for any table at all.

But this criticism scarcely hits the mark with regard to Koheleth. He was not an unbridled sensualist, nor was he a drunkard, though teetotallers may chide him for refreshing himself with wine. A drunkard or a lecherous sensualist could never have carried out his vast building schemes, his architectural gardening, his afforestation, his collecting of things of beauty, luxury and civilisation, his patronage of the arts, with such perfection and regal magnificence. All this requires ideas, purpose, energy and taste, and the very worst we can say about it is, that it is Oriental. But consider a man in a similar position to-day. He is left a magnificent property and a vast fortune. With the help of his fortune he improves his estate, lays out the gardens in luxuriant beauty, plants trees in waste places, forms ponds where the trout dart swiftly, has much glass where flowers of tropical beauty blossom and choicest fruits ripen, turns the old place of his fathers into a paradise ; a man of taste, he collects pictures by the masters, has choicest tapestries veiling his walls, and on his table precious treasures in gold and silver, the cunning work of deftest skill. Philanthropists might say with so much poverty in the world he could spend his money in more needed ways ; Socialists may call him a bloated plutocrat ; but he is not because of his wealth, magnificence, and taste a sinner before God above all the sons of men. What

Pessimism and Love

a day he might give you showing you his spacious gardens, his laden vines, his ancient woods and shooting trees, his treasures of art, feeding you with a chaste luxury that turns eating into a fine art, and then at the close of the day calling his master of music (a chorus of men and women singers were too Oriental) to let you hear the deep diapasons and the seraphic *vox humana* of his organ, specified and built by Willis of London. It would be a day to remember and talk about in your waking hours and to dream of in your sleep. Are you a philanthropist? (let us hope you are), you would want to take your particular *protégés*, your Sunday school, or your slum children, or your working lads to sport for a day in the parks, to walk round the gardens and see the wonders of luxury and beauty. Are you a Socialist? you would only need to have an open invitation for a visit at any time to find your ideas on wealth and property undergoing slight modifications, and only need to be made heir-presumptive of the estate, to find you had quite definite views on the rights of the land and the landlord. Philanthropist, Socialist, Individualist, Tory or Radical, Conformist or Nonconformist, whatever you are, you are human, and on the modern Koheleth would probably pronounce a quite human judgment and call him a favourite of fortune or a lucky fellow.

But there was a fly in the ointment that made this pleasant and luxurious life distasteful and even nauseous. What was it? Was it the unadulterated sensuousness? Was it the making of pleasure the one and only god? Would Koheleth have saved himself much disappointment and chagrin if he had added a mental discipline to his sensuous enjoyment, or if,

The Experiment with Pleasure

instead of living a life devoted to pleasure, he had chosen the sterner path of scientific and intellectual pursuits ? It happens that one of our own poets has given us a picture of a life which, while it did not disdain the æsthetic and pleasurable, gave due consideration to the claims of intellect and reason—a picture which well answers these questions. The lordly pleasure house which Tennyson in his poem " The Palace of Art " depicts the soul as building, is a temple, not only of art and pleasure, but of the intellect and reason. In that palace there were not only " courts with their squared lawns," " dragons spouting from their golden gorge," " cloisters branched like mighty woods "—all things to delight the eye and charm the senses, but

" There was Milton like a seraph strong,
 Beside him Shakespeare bland and mild ;
And there the world-worn Dante grasped his song
 And somewhat grimly smiled.

. . . . .

" And thro' the topmost Oriels' coloured flame
 Two god-like faces gazed below ;
Plato the wise, and large-browed Verulam,
 The first of those who know."

The silent faces of the great and wise were there, making their appeal and giving inspiration. But all this intellectual reinforcement did not make the building an unsullied joy and satisfaction. The lordly pleasure-house proved to be " a white elephant." The soul that built it was sick of it, and its " intellectual throne."

Pessimism and Love

" Three years
She prospered : on the fourth she fell
Like Herod, when the shout was in his ears,
Struck thro' with pangs of hell.

．　　．　　．　　．　　．

" When she would think, where'er she turned her sight
The airy hand confusion wrought,
Wrote ' Mene, mene,' and divided quite
The kingdom of her thought."

The building of the pleasure-house, in spite of the place given to reason and intellect in it, was vanity and pursuit after wind. And even if Koheleth had given more honour to the great and wise, if he had sat at the feet of Moses and the prophets, or at the feet of Plato and Aristotle and the Cynics and Cyrenaics of Greece, if, amidst his pleasant surroundings, he had been a student of Hebrew lore or Greek philosophy, if he in his most lordly pleasure-house had raised an intellectual throne, he would still have cried out, " The whole is vanity and a pursuit after wind."

Was it perhaps that there were no forms or exercises of religion, no offices of prayer and praise, in this most pleasurable enterprise ? Well ; Koheleth might have built a chapel in his domains and engaged a private chaplain to give thanks to God for the blessings of this life that had come to the feudal lord and his dependants, and for those possibly greater blessings that might come in the future. The chaplain no doubt would have been well paid and most punctilious in his duties ; but, I am afraid, Koheleth would have voted him a dull fellow whose reading of prayers led one to deep

The Experiment with Pleasure

meditation on the vanity of existence. Or he might have taken to religion of another form. He might have read his Bible, the prophets with their glowing descriptions of a new and better order of society and their prophecies of a Day of the Lord when that which was crooked would be made straight and that which was lacking could be numbered; or the psalmists with their deep trust in God and His help. But he probably would have said these prophetic hopes and ideals, two or four or even six centuries old, are not yet realised; the Day of the Lord has as yet no promise of its coming; their ideals are but empty visions and themselves visionaries following after vanity and pursuing the wind; and the trust of the psalmists has not been justified, for the righteous still suffer and have no better lot than the wicked. Or he might have set himself on some approved prescription to secure the salvation of his soul, and so have had now the delights of this world and in the future those of a world to come; but alas, poor fellow! he was not sure that he had a soul to save at all, and to labour to save a soul whose existence is uncertain would be like jumping into the sea to save a drowning man who was not there—that would be a vanity and a pursuit after water. In a word, it is doubtful whether any religious exercise or zeal thrown into this life of gorgeous pleasantness would have altered his feeling or his judgment. It would still be a vanity and a pursuit after wind.

What *was* the fly in the ointment? Plainly there was one, a particularly poisonous one, that could spread disease and corruption over life with such pleasurable possibilities, that could turn all the profusions of wealth and luxury into nauseating carrion. The fly is there,

Pessimism and Love

writ large on the printed page—there in the Hebrew Bible, in the English Bible, in every Bible. A score of capital "I's" in eleven short verses ! That capital " I " is the fly, the " I " of a blatant egotism, the " I " of a colossal selfhood, the " I " of an absolute selfishness. Koheleth was an ego-maniac.

It was the same with the soul, the intellectual soul, that built its lordly pleasure-house, and the poet has not concealed the destructive creature.

> " My soul would live alone unto herself
> In her high palace there."

> " She took her throne :
> She sat betwixt the shining Oriels,
> To sing her songs alone."

She boasted in her god-like isolation. Her boast was her doom. Æsthetic, intellectual, the worshipper of reason and the arts, like Koheleth she was a mighty egotist. She built her temple for herself, and it proved her undoing and her curse.

This mighty egotism is not usually given as the cause of Koheleth's failure. It is said that he plunged too deeply into pleasure ; he broke the law of temperance in all things, of moderation, of "nothing too much." But he did impose a certain restriction upon his desires, and even if he had imposed it more stringently, it is very doubtful whether his disappointment would have been less. He would have felt the restriction itself as a pain and as a spoiling of his pleasure. It is quite true that excess in pleasure leads to the fulness of satiety and pleasure becomes almost a pain ; quite true, that if a man rushes through life, desiring too

The Experiment with Pleasure

much, wishing strongly and greedily to taste life in one draught thoroughly, not gleaning or tasting it, but tearing it like a bunch of grapes, crushing and twisting it, he will remain with stained hands and thirst unquenched. But it is just as true that if a man turns his back on life and its joys, trying not to desire at all, refusing to taste one single delight, turning to the wilderness where no grapes are, trying to make existence a mighty negation, he too will know the fulness of satiety, void and empty fulness though it be, and will thirst with a great thirst for life. No mere measuring of the quantity of pleasure that can be legitimately enjoyed—even though the measurement be the sternest moderation—can save from the sickening disappointment and the mournful conclusion that all is vanity and a pursuit after wind. It is quite true, too, that Koheleth made pleasure the chief end and all of life, tried to turn life into pleasure and pleasure alone, and that in this he made a false choice of the end of man. Man is not built for pleasure alone.

" Not for this
Was common clay ta'en from the common earth,
Moulded by God and tempered with the tears
Of angels to the perfect shape of man."

Man is not simply built to be a pleasure-consumer, and where he tries to be one he is going against the very constitution and purpose of his life. But no more was he built to be a simple pain-bearing machine; not for pain alone was " common clay ta'en from the common earth." Pain and pleasure are themselves parts of the common earth, and the egotist may take either or both,

Pessimism and Love

and other things too, but whatever he takes he will model but a misshapen vessel. Whatever he works in, the egotist is a poor craftsman in life.

Koheleth never learnt the secret of his blunder as the soul that built the lordly pleasure-house in Tennyson's poem did.

> " So when four years were wholly finished,
>   She threw her royal robes away.
>   ' Make me a cottage in the vale,' she said,
>   ' Where I may mourn and pray.
>
> " ' Yet pull not down my palace towers, that are
>   So lightly, beautifully built :
>   Perchance I may return with others there
>   When I have purged my guilt.' "

The palace towers were not sinful. No more were Koheleth's great possessions. It was the selfish isolation, the exclusiveness, the egotism, that were the sin and the failure. Let others be taken into the pleasure, the knowledge and the beauty of life that may be ours, and then these will not be vanity.

> " He that shuts love out in turn shall be
>   Shut out from love and on her threshold lie,
>   Howling in outer darkness."

Man is " ta'en from the common earth," not to seek his own pleasure, nor to cultivate his own intellect, nor to save his soul, but he is taken to lose his life, to give it away, its pleasure, its knowledge, its beauty—to give it all away that he may save all.

THE DIVINE PROGRAMME

Every thing has its appointed day, and every business beneath the heavens has its time.

> There is a time to be born,
> And a time to die.
> There is a time to plant,
> And a time to uproot.
> There is a time to wound,
> And a time to bind the wounded.
> There is a time to break down,
> And a time to build up.
> There is a time to weep,
> And a time to laugh.
> There is a time to lament,
> And a time to dance.
> There is a time to cast stones away,
> And a time to gather stones.
> There is a time to embrace,
> And a time to refrain from embracing.
> There is a time to seek,
> And a time to lose.
> There is a time to keep,
> And a time to cast away.

Pessimism and Love

> There is a time to rend,
>   And a time to sew together.
> There is a time to be silent,
>   And a time to speak.
> There is a time to love,
>   And a time to hate.
> There is a time of war,
>   And a time of peace.
>
> What reward hath the worker for all his toil ? I have seen the work which God hath given to the sons of men for their busy occupation.
>
> CHAP. III. 1—10.

These words are usually regarded as a description of the orderliness of existence and as an exhortation to timeliness. There is a time for everything, so let everything be in its time. Punctuality is here put into poetry (for the passage is poetic in form at least). And no doubt timeliness is an excellent and effective virtue ; a poetic virtue indeed, for it makes as much for the beauty as for the usefulness of life. Timeliness in common speech, for instance, is better than an angel's tongue in perpetual motion, and nearly all the well-intentioned stupidities of life, that bring so much harm, are due to their simple unseasonableness. If we could only be timely in everything, we should be well on our way to realising the old Stoic command of living according to Nature (ὁμολογουμένως τῇ φύσει ζῆν) and to making life a thing of beauty and real effectiveness. However, I have no intention of adding an untimely sermon to the many timely ones that this

The Divine Programme

passage has inspired, for the simple reason that timeliness does not happen to be the theme here. The idea of the pessimist is not of the seasonableness of everything and of the wisdom of seasonable action, but rather of the fixed order of all human experience. Every part and parcel of our life's experience has its fixed dates, everything is preordained, the programme of life is all drawn up and all the events happen to the minute. That is his thought, and it leads him again to the pessimistic conclusion that all is vanity and a pursuit after wind. In effect, the pessimist is here presenting us with our life's programme written with an iron pen in indelible ink. We may not like the programme, we might like to change or omit an item or two, but that is impossible; we have to take it all exactly as it is drawn up to time, and sit through it from the opening selection to the national anthem. Should we request a slight alteration in the order of events, as being more in consonance with our moods, the chairman is inexorable, the programme must be gone through just as it stands. That may be taking the poetry out of the passage; it may be acting like a Philistine : it is; but even a Philistine has his rights, the right to state the truth in his own language. And the truth is that it is not the beauty of timeliness, but the iron of fatalism that we have here, æsthetically worked up (the Philistine will concede) into poetry. And, like all fatalism, it leads to the fatalistic conclusion that all is vanity and a pursuit after wind, for what is the use of trying to change life, if all its experiences are timed to take place at fixed, unchangeable moments?

Now this passage is interesting from the fact that in it are interposed comments from the pietist and the

Pessimism and Love

hedonist. The pietist does not deny the fatalism; he accepts the fixedness of human experience. But he says the Author of it is God, and that God has made it all beautiful, and He has made it all in its unalterableness that men may fear Him. God is the Author of the programme, but it is an artistic programme, though it may be also somewhat fearsome. While the fixed order reduces the pessimist to despair, it inspires the pietist with fear with a dash of æsthetic feeling in it. But it is very questionable whether the pietist has much moral advantage. As emotions, fear and despair are closely akin, neither of them can be regarded as a fountain of inspiration for the living of life. Even though we give to the fear the highest value and regard it as reverence in face of a beautiful, unalterable order of existence, the pietist is still a fatalist, in spite of his religion and æsthetic feeling. Piety does not remove the iron and indelible ink of the passage. The hedonist (v. 12) as little denies the fatalism. He solves it, however, by making the best of it. There are good things on the programme, eating and drinking and pleasuring one's self and getting happiness out of one's work. Well; take these. On the programmes presented to some individuals there may be quite a number of these things, quite enough to make the entertainment as a whole very pleasant and agreeable. But if the pleasant things on the programme are not very numerous, the hedonistic solution, in that case, would be but cold comfort. And even if the programme were from beginning to end agreeable to hedonistic taste, it is doubtful whether human nature would even in such pleasant circumstances be satisfied, for we do like to be able to say, " No, thank you," even to our

The Divine Programme

pleasures. We object to be made the mere creatures of pleasure, and it is questionable whether necessitated pleasure would be pleasure at all. It is on the fatalism that we stick and cannot away with it. We would rather be free and miserable than happy and in bondage, and both pietist and hedonist, in spite of their solutions, leave us slaves.

Can we challenge the fatalism ? Can we confidently deny it ? That is the real question. Well ; we must confess that there *is* a programme and most of the events are fixed. There is a time to be born and there is a time to die, and few of us have much say in either. There is a time to be young and there is a time to be old, and any attempt to change them is a piece of futile folly. There is a time to weep and a time to laugh, and the times for laughter and tears are not at our bidding. There *is* a programme of life with the chief events absolutely fixed ; there is an order to which our experience simply has to conform ; necessarianism covers a large part of human existence. There is truth in the pessimist's statement that to everything there is an appointed time. But there is no need on that ground for pessimistic fatalism. Suppose there were no prearranged programme of life ; suppose that every mortal had to arrange his own programme. In that case overwhelming difficulty would meet us at the very threshold, for it would need a good deal of courage to say, " Now is my time to be born and I will be born."

But let us try to imagine that that initial difficulty is overcome, and on our own initiative we have made the plunge into existence. We have arrived, let us say, and the programme is absolutely blank in our hands. What are we to be or do next ? What bit of human

Pessimism and Love

experience are we to lay hold of ? Laughter at the hopeless blank might seem the most natural ; but one can scarcely laugh at nothing, and to raise a genuine laugh we should have to gather comic or ridiculous elements together, a task which at the time might prove so difficult as to knock all the laughter out of us, and even if we succeeded with more or less ease, the laughter would not be genuine, but very forced and artificial. Well, what next ? Let us have a weep. A perfectly voluntary weep is, to say the least, a slightly hypocritical procedure. But, after all, weeping and laughter are minor considerations. Having arrived, we should have to fix the time of youth, middle life and old age ; nay, we should have to fix the time when we should be eighteen and when we should be forty-three. We should have in such circumstances a very strange world : new arrivals with hoary locks and bent with age, veterans in their teens, and the whole world of humans moving forwards and backwards in time, jumping from moment to moment at their own caprice, so that nobody would know at what point of time he or anybody else was. In a word, we should all be in hopeless, haphazard, chaotic confusion. If we had any sense left, we should be crying out for order, for a fixed programme, and the more fixed the better. We should be thankful that there is a programme at all, that arrangements have been made for the carrying out of life, for, to say the least, it saves us a vast amount of trouble. There is a fixed order of life which makes life an orderly thing.

But does this order condemn us to absolutely necessitated existence ? Does it turn us into slaves ? To answer that question we must examine the order, we

The Divine Programme

must study our programmes. If there were only one event on the programme, say, to sit still and look into vacancy, we should be slaves, or even if there were half a dozen events—a time to sleep and a time to wake, a time to eat and a time to drink, a time to stand and a time to sit down—we should still be slaves, and no accumulation of events of that kind would give us freedom. But, looking through our fixed times, we see that they are of such a nature as to call forth and develop the powers of our personality, our thought, our feeling, our conscience.

We do not sit still, dumb and passive, under the order, but we enter into it and into all its events, and in so doing we rise to the stature of our manhood; we enlarge our experience, we grow in personality and its powers. The order is one suited to us and we are suited to it. It is an education making for efficiency in the fullest sense of the term. It develops in us a rich and unified personality in which various emotions, many intellectual activities, and moral powers find their place. In a word, the order makes us men and women. With such an order, with such a programme presented to us, all is not vanity nor a pursuit after wind.

Within the order of life's experience there is a perfect freedom, that is, a freedom to develop along the line of perfection. We do not and we cannot fix the time to be born and the time to die, the time to plant and the time to gather, the time to laugh and the time to weep; but these times are not barred doors impeding our progress, but open avenues inviting us to a larger and richer experience. We may refuse to enter. It may be a time to plant and we may say we will not plant. We may, as we think, assert our freedom, but what in such case we are really doing is this—we are

Pessimism and Love

denying ourselves, refusing to enter into the freedom of a larger experience. The fixed times, the order of existence, the programme presented to us, are not the limitations of life, but its great opportunities.

There is another way of looking at the order. The times are fixed—the time to be born and the time to die, with all the intermediate moments. But the character of the times, their moral quality and content, depends upon ourselves. There is a time to laugh ; we do not fix it, we are not responsible for it, but we are responsible for the manner of our laughter, for its moral quality and character. Whether we laugh with a gladness that is almost praise or with a cachinnation, in which the grating ingredients of discontent and grudge are plainly manifest—well, that depends on the spirit which we have made for ourselves. There is a time to die, but a man may die in Christ or in miserable despair. The character of death depends upon ourselves. In simple words, the programme is presented to us, all the events in order, and we can either make it a misery and a failure or a glorious success.

The pessimist puts the programme into poetry. Its wonderful variety inspires him. The pietist, too, feels the beauty of it. And as we think of the programme, its perfect orderliness, its countless events, the infinite variety of them, each one a great opportunity, we feel the orderliness, the beauty, the richness of life, and it is only poetry that can speak of these things. The programme is a great poem. It is a programme created by Love, and presented to the sons of men that they may share the orderliness, the beauty, the wealth of life of its Author—that they may share the immortal life and be sons of God.

MAN AND BEAST

And further. I have perceived beneath the sun, that in the place of judgment there is iniquity and in the place of righteousness there is iniquity.—CHAP. III. 16.

And I said in mine heart, this is because of the sons of men, to prove them hath God done it, and that they may see that they are beasts, simply beasts. For (mere) chance are the sons of men, and chance are the beasts, there is the same chance to them both : as one dieth, so dieth the other ; and one spirit is to all, and the advantage of man over the beasts is nothing, for the whole is vanity. All go to one place ; all are from the dust and all return to the dust. Who knoweth the spirit of the sons of men whether it goeth upward and the spirit of the beasts whether it goeth downward to the earth ?—CHAP. III. 18—21.

What Koheleth says here is quite unmistakable, and quite modern in its agnosticism and in its absolute materialism. Man and beast are alike : they have one spirit ; they are made of one and the same stuff—the dust of the earth ; their destiny is the same ; dust they both are and to dust they return ; for who knoweth

Pessimism and Love

the spirit of the sons of men, whether it goeth upward, or the spirit of the beast, whether it goeth downward ? If any one should risk an opinion, it is a pure guess. No one knows. That is quite unmistakable in meaning, and quite modern, quite up-to-date, and very like something we read only yesterday or may read to-morrow.

Koheleth, however, does not come to the conclusion that man and beast are one in the same way as the moderns. He sees in the society of his day very few, if any, signs of a moral order (v. 16) ; man is governed, apparently, much by the same laws of selfishness, cunning and greed as govern the animals, and so he concludes that man and beast are the same. The moderns say that man and beast are the same, in the sacred name of evolution and the demonstrated facts of science. Koheleth and the moderns start from different premises, but they both arrive at the same conclusion—a conclusion which is neither complimentary nor flattering to mankind. Man is separated by no greater structural barrier from the brutes than they are from one another. From the structure of the manlike ape, from similarity in the greater organs, from the skull and cranial capacity, from hand and foot and teeth, from texture and size of the brain, the ape might be called the older form of man. That is the modern way of saying that man and beast are of one spirit and of one dust. Man is made out to be a very near blood-relation of the ape. He is an animal, highly organised, variously and infinitely developed, a refined, trained, and educated animal, but an animal and nothing more. Man and ape are of one dust and have one spirit.

Man and Beast

Now the similarities between a man and an ape are obvious enough. One does not need to be a man of science to perceive them. In any zoological gardens there are apes marvellously like men, and, outside the gardens, some men with more than shadowy resemblances to the ape. But how really stands the case between man and the ape ? Here is a manlike ape. He comes probably of an older ancestry than man ; he can boast a longer lineage. Perhaps he was thousands of years on this globe before ever man appeared. But consider him a little. He is still very much like his most ancient ancestor. He is engaged very much in the same business and conducts it on the same most ancient methods. He gathers and cracks his nuts just in the same way as his most remote ancestor did. He has not forged for himself a pair of nut-crackers to save his teeth. He practises the same arboreal architecture. He has not discovered the superiority of slates or tiles or thatch for a roof. He indulges himself in the ancient gymnastics, swinging himself from tree to tree like his ancestor. He emits shrieks of ferocity and alarm which no one could possibly call musical. What he was in the far distant unknown past he still is. He was a brute then ; he is a brute still.

Now consider man. He may have been in the dim, remote, unknown pages of history an ape, or very like an ape. He may have dwelt in holes and caves beneath the ground. But he did not continue to dwell there. He built for himself hut and house and palatial mansion ; he has built temples that are a wonder and a glory to his skill ; he has gathered himself into cities where commerce and art and culture abound. He has formed words, and

Pessimism and Love

out of words tongues, and out of tongues literatures that seem immortal. He has looked on the face of Nature and seen Nature's beauty and transferred it to canvas that became as wondrous almost as Nature herself. He has penetrated Nature's secrets and bound her discovered forces to his chariot, which passes over earth and sea and through the air. He has turned his heart to the unseen and the unknown and found in the unseen and unknown a Spirit like his own spirit, only infinite and eternal. Man that was once so low in the scale has won for himself kingdoms of knowledge, literature, art and religion. He may have been like an ape once; he has become something like a god.

Between man and the ape there are great worlds, infinite gulfs, and he who can say man is a beast, and that they are of one spirit, must be blind and deaf and dumb, incapable of making any distinctions at all.

Suppose that man and ape were absolutely similar in structure, in nervous organism, in brain tissue, then man, who is so different in knowledge, in art, in politics, in religion, in everything that really counts in the scale of worth and greatness, only becomes the greater miracle. The same in structure! but infinitely different in mind, in heart, in will, in reason, in soul. That is the miracle. The ape and man were born alike. But man had a future. That future made the infinite difference, the everlasting distinction between them. Consider man and beast, and what strikes you, when you are thinking sense at all, is the simply unspeakable, unthinkable difference they present!

It may be said that some animals show a considerable

Man and Beast

intelligence, which, under training, can be greatly increased. They do. Sea-lions, for instance, can perform wonderful feats of skill, which are quite beyond the power of most theologians, philosophers, poets, and even of scientists. They can balance quick-revolving globes upon their snouts, catch from a distance of twenty yards haddocks in their mouths with never a slip, and even dance round the ring to the strains of a dreamy waltz. They can, supported by the band, go through a toy-symphony, but what it would exactly sound like without the assistance of the human orchestra words would fail to describe. They have a most wonderful intelligence, but not one tenth part of the intelligence of their lord and master who makes these brutes go through their antics ; for if they had, they would float a circus on their own account and, for their own account, secure the not-to-be-despised profits of the show. Some people go into exaggerated rapture at such performance. It is to them the most wonderful thing under the sun. At such rapture one naturally asks the question if they have ever heard of *Hamlet*, or, supposing they have, if they have ever suspected a sea-lion or any other lion as its author (the authorship has been disputed), or even one of these wonderful beasts reading *Hamlet* for his own delectation and profit.

Some parrots specialise in music. They can, shall we say, sing ? a psalm or a verse of a hymn ; but it is doubtful, even if the day of the precentor were not past, whether the most musical, intellectual, and pious parrot would ever, even by a most unmusical congregation, be entrusted to lead the praise of the sanctuary. What are the raucous shrieks or even the most liquid notes of birds compared with the productions of

Pessimism and Love

harmonious sound, a symphony of Beethoven, the stirring melody of a folk-song, or the strains of a common hymn !

Dogs especially are supposed to develop a high order of intelligence. They are allowed to have the rudiments of a conscience. Robert Louis Stevenson tells the story—quite a delightful story it is—of a dog that was addicted to the offence of sheep worrying ; but evidently it had some conscience on the matter, for it was in the habit, after a marauding enterprise, of going to the river to wash off the gory marks of the fray. It felt a deep remorse. It had a conscience. A conscience ! a very cunning conscience indeed. But can one imagine a dog grieving with a deep sorrow over sins that could never be found out, the secret sins of the heart, striving to overcome them, not because of any penalty attached to them, but just because they are sins before heaven and before God ? Some dogs have even more than the rudiments of conscience—they have the instincts of religion ; they know when the day of rest comes round, know better how to behave on it than some humans ; but can one imagine the canine race, with a mighty spiritual daring, breaking the bars of time, piercing " the ramparts of the world," forcing themselves by faith and vision into the unseen and the eternal, and claiming a place, an inheritance, and a home there ?

Yes, animals are wonderful; they have about them the wonder of creation and the Creator's skill; but though they were, in their own way and on their own lines, far more wonderful than they are and more capable of feats of strength and agility and cunning and, we may say, intelligence than they are, they would still not be the equal of man nor belong to the

Man and Beast

order of man's life and existence. Even if the well-known tradition that the cow jumped over the moon be authentic, this feat would not make her the equal or bring her into the same order of life as the man who sits in his observatory, and who with eye and telescope has seen the surface of the moon, noted its valleys and hills, has watched the stars in their gliding flight, and, though he may be at almost infinite distance away, has actually lived in thought in that vast ether field, whence the light came to us half a million of years ago. Strength, agility, cunning, these are not the measures of greatness, but mind, heart, reason, and soul with the worlds of thought, beauty, love, and religion in which they live, these point the true glory and these belong to man ; and so far are they with their worlds above anything in the animal kingdom, that we can say, speaking from the simple facts, man is not a beast ; they are not of one dust, still less are they of the same spirit. Man is a son of God and of the eternal ; the beast is a creature of time and space.

But in one point at least man and beast are alike. They are both subject to death and decay. In death they are not divided. "Who knoweth the spirit of the sons of men, whether it goeth upward, or the spirit of the beast, whether it goeth downward ?" A sceptical question, a cynical question, an atheistical question perhaps; but in the very asking of it man shows his infinite removal from the beast, for it is a question which the beast never asks, with which its reason is never exercised, nor its heart ever troubled, and the very asking reveals that death is not the same to man as to beast. To beast death is no problem; to man it is the heaviest problem of all. Death to the

Pessimism and Love

beast is just death ; to man it is at least a mighty possibility. To the beast it is the end, if it is anything at all ; to man it is a gateway into darkness or into light.

But who knoweth whether the spirit of a man goeth upward ? We can answer, The man of thought knows, the man who has looked upon the long history of his race, from the lowly beginnings to the present greatness, and felt an eternal future to be a rational necessity, the only reasonable completion and consummation of this long history ; he knows that the spirit of man has already risen upwards and is full of promise of a yet higher rise. Or the man who has considered man's marvellous capacities for knowing, for thinking, for feeling and for right doing, and feels that not yet, not in this world, have these powers come to their own and their achievements been fully completed, feels that they require another and larger existence for their true exercise and complete development—he knows. Or the man who has listened to the voice of his own soul, claiming a freedom and a joy that this world cannot give, and who has heard the echoes of the same voice coming from the heart of his fellows—he knows. The man who is true to his reason and fair to the best aspirations of his heart knows that immortality is a necessity to mind and soul.

But yet all that the reason and heart can give is probability, a high degree of probability, that man is immortal, but only probability after all. Immortality cannot be absolutely proved. It can be assumed on strong grounds of the reason ; it can be regarded as a necessary hypothesis without which life would be meaningless, but when all is said there remains only the greatest measure of probability. Well ; we can take the

Man and Beast

probability at the bidding of the reason. We can live as though we were immortal, and the reason and the soul back us up, if we may so say, in the endeavour. Immortality is not only a rational hypothesis, it is a noble one, and adopting it bravely we shall not live less nobly. Our thoughts will not be less pure, lofty, and ideal because we assume the motions of our mind continue for ever; our love will not be less kind because we believe the pulses of our heart are eternal, nor will our actions be less worthy because we have assumed that they, in their essential being, abide and make an eternal character. If we assume that man lives for ever, we are not at least an ill bird fouling its own nest, like those who say "Man is a beast and dieth like the beasts of the field."

Does even still the voice of scepticism arise saying "Who knows? who knows?" We can yet hearken to another voice speaking in unhesitating acts and saying "We know that if the earthly house of our tabernacle be dissolved, we have a building from God, a house not made with hands, eternal, in the heavens." We know—we that be risen in Christ and in whose hearts Christ is risen, we who are now living His immortal life of service and love—we know we do not die. They, in whose heart heaven is now, know that they are in heaven for ever. Who knows? Christ knows. He does not reason, nor argue, nor speculate. He knows, and out of His certain knowledge says, "In My Father's House are many mansions." And he to whom Christ is the life of his life, mind of his mind, heart of his heart, soul of his soul, he knows, and with no unfaltering accents can say, "Blessed are the dead that die in the Lord."

THE BED-ROCK OF PESSIMISM

And again, I considered all the oppressions which exist beneath the sun; and see, (what is there but) the tears of the oppressed! and they have no comforter. On the side of the oppressors there is power, but the oppressed have no comforter. And I congratulated the dead who are already dead, rather than the living who are still alive. And more than both of them is to be congratulated he who hath not yet been and hath not seen the evil work that is done beneath the sun.—CHAP. IV. 1—3.

Better is the day of one's death than the day of one's birth.—CHAP. VII. 1*b*.

Koheleth has turned his attention to the oppressions which men suffer at the hands of their fellows—to man's inhumanity to man; he has seen the tears and afflictions of the oppressed, has noted that they have none to defend or comfort them, and that force and power are on the side of the strong and the oppressor. The sight has so saddened and sickened him that he declares that the dead are more fortunate than the living, not indeed because they are in a more felicitous state, but just because they are dead, finally and completely finished with life. He goes further and says, that more fortunate than either dead or living are those who have never seen the light nor known the evil of existence.

The Bed-rock of Pessimism

Life is really a curse and a positive evil. Non-existence is better than existence. Not to be at all, is a more fortunate lot than to be. That is the bed-rock of pessimism. No one could sink into a deeper despair of life.

Now one might judge this desperate pessimism to be but the expression of a hopeless mood ; the ebullition of a heart overflowing with a temporary bitterness, or perhaps the spitting forth of an unworthy spite against the conditions of life. If it were that, it might deserve pity, perhaps scorn and mere contempt. But there are facts which prevent us from pronouncing too hastily an offhand, or pitiful or contemptuous, judgment on this bed-rock pessimism. For one thing, it is full of compassion. He considered the oppressed, their tears and their helplessness ; he saw man's inhumanity to man in all its tragic effects, beheld it with its blood-red harvest of human suffering, and he was moved to compassion. He was plunged into a profound pity, into a despair born of sympathy with the sufferings of humanity. And any mood or conviction that arises out of so divine and human a thing as compassion deserves thoughtful and sympathetic consideration. For another thing, Koheleth does not stand alone in this absolute pessimism, in this hopeless despair of human existence, which even breaks forth amidst the gaiety and love of life of the ancient Greeks.

" Best lot for man is never to be born,
    Nor ever seen the bright rays of the morn :
    Next best, when born, to haste with quickest tread,
    Where Hades' gates are open for the dead,
    And rest with much earth gathered for our bed."

Pessimism and Love

And, further, it was this same pity for the woe of humanity that led Buddha to the same pessimistic conclusion—set forth in his doctrine of *Nirvana*, a doctrine which declares absolute annihilation to be the one desirable thing, and that not-being is better than being ; and one may be sure of this, that a doctrine which has attracted millions has at least some foundation. And the same voice of despair has been uttered in our own day, a voice coming, not out of the mysterious East, but out of the excitement, prosperity, and glory of our Western civilisation. Schopenhauer is a name well known ; he is popular, the people read him—or did—and, though he may not be an attractive personality, his name has a place in the history of great thinkers. He had the same pity (amongst other less desirable qualities) as Koheleth and the same despair of life. Tolstoy, the Russian, had a touch of the same despair, and our own Lord Byron had a pessimistic hatred of life. Koheleth does not stand alone in his pessimism. We may not endorse the pessimistic judgment. We may scorn it, pity it, ridicule it ; we may call it morbid, false, atheistic, but perhaps if we had more imagination, a wider and deeper sympathy for the sorrows, trials, and tragedies of life, we should at least be gentle and forgiving to a despair born of compassion and the oppressions of the oppressed.

But if, after making due allowance for the cause of this pessimism, we adjudge it to be morbid, false, and atheistic, we may then ask the question whether it is worthy of consideration, whether by healthy minds it should not receive summary and instant dismissal and be flung out of our view of things, as some hideous spectre that by its very presence seems wantonly to

The Bed-rock of Pessimism

spoil the beauty and joy of life. Is pessimism worth a moment's thought ? Evidently the Bible thinks it is, for it is here in all its bed-rock blackness ; and if we ask why the Bible gives it a place, we might answer that the Bible is as broad in its survey as human life, shuts its eyes to no facts that have anything like universality ; and pessimism is one of the facts of life, appearing again and again in history, raising its miserable and hopeless countenance, like some ghost of blackest night, amidst every kind of civilisation, and blighting with its sunless gaze much that is fair and beautiful.

We often say that we are not superstitious and do not believe in ghosts; but if there should be report of a ghost, the best way to disbelieve in it is to find it out, go up to it and grip it, and just learn what the ghastly thing really is. If we do not run away from it, but go up quietly to it and lay hands upon it, we shall never believe in that particular ghost again. It is in some such way that the Bible treats this ghastly pessimism. It is not afraid of it ; it does not shut its eyes to the sight of it nor its ears to the report of it ; it lets it come on to show itself in the open ; admits it into its pages, to reveal itself there in its actual, naked reality. And that is the most courageous and satisfactory manner of dealing with all pessimism, whether of Koheleth, or Schopenhauer, or any other—to face it, to touch, handle, and examine it, to see whether it has reality and truth or is but the ghastly apparition of a pathologically diseased brain. Do not simply hurl stones at it, calling it a gospel of despair, or an atheistical creed, or a paralysing faith : it may be ; but the stones do not hurt the pessimism, it rather likes them, as increasing

Pessimism and Love

the sum of human miseries. Rather, have the courage of the Bible. Face pessimism. Grip it and test its reality.

Let us face this creed: "The world had better never have been; life is a positive evil and a curse." Let us try to answer the pessimist. Well; if that creed be accepted, the very obvious thing for the believer in it is to get out of this world by the nearest and easiest door. He need not have Hamlet's hesitation—" the dread of something after death," or of the " dreams that may come when we have shuffled off this mortal coil," for the pessimist has no " something after death," and if he had, it could not be worse than this present existence, which is to him the bottom abyss of evil and misery. The entertainment provided in this world is a misery and positive pain. But he is not chained to his seat, and the doors of the theatre are not locked. He can easily leave his place; the doors will yield to the gentlest pressure and he can walk out. He can remove himself. As a consistent pessimist he ought to do so. In an absolutely hopeless and wretched world, suicide is not merely justifiable, it is the right thing. But pessimists do not commit suicide. They keep their seats, perhaps to enjoy the consoling and even luxurious refreshments occasionally served out in life's entertainment, or to comfort others with their own misery, (this motive may seem very self-sacrificing to pessimists themselves, but the sacrifice is quite thrown away, for " they'd none of 'em be missed "), or to get the full pleasure out of their own painful existence. They find some excuse to stay on to the last act when the curtain drops and the lights are put out,

The Bed-rock of Pessimism

and they have to go from the theatre of life, whether they will or no.

Pessimists preach, but they practise not. They condemn the drama with their lips, but by their action of sitting on pay it the highest compliment. Other men applaud the acts, pessimists only hiss as soon as the curtain is raised, hiss till it drops, and as they do not leave their seats of their own accord and say they dislike the play, we can only conclude that they sit it out because they like to hiss; hissing is their life and evidently a pleasant occupation to them. If pessimists were to act consistently with their creed, they would leave the theatre at once. If they were to make their creed consistent with their action and circumstances, they would really be optimists. They like hissing, and though hissing is not particularly polite nor a special mark of high breeding, it is not criminal, and so they get what they like. The world gives them their desire. They ought to be glorious optimists. Hissing is the realisation of the ideal to them and they realise it. What more can they want out of the world?

Pessimism is not only a condemnation of life, it is a charge against God. It arraigns the justice and love of the Creator; it says that He is guilty of creating an evil thing. It is a denial of all we mean by the word "God." A distinguished expositor calls this very section of Ecclesiastes "A polemic against the teaching of the Righteousness of the Divine Providence." Pessimism is a polemic against God. It is a denial of His justice and love. It is practically and really atheism. It denies God in the world. But that does not help the evil, and the

Pessimism and Love

pain, and the suffering in the world. Take God, eternal goodness and love out of the world, you do not improve the world nor increase its hope. Without God in the world, then without hope. With God living, active, healing, saving, redeeming in the world, then there is hope, hope that out of all the sum of evil and pain good may be brought. God is the one hope in a world where there is suffering and pain and woe and misery beyond the power of man to alleviate or remove. If only Koheleth had seen God, God in the world loving and righteous, he would have seen the oppressions of the oppressed and their tears, but he would not have said they had no comforter. His sky would not have been utterly black. If he had seen God he would not only have seen the tears of the oppressed, but One trying to dry them, and he, too, would have tried to wipe the tears from their eyes. The oppressed would have had a comforter and he himself would have been a happier man.

Pessimists they are with their lips, with their lips only, and a creed that is of the lips alone and never inspires more than a lip-service is a ghost, a ghastly apparition. The best way to treat it is to grip it with a firm grip.

It is scarcely fair, however, to judge a creed by its professors and their inconsistencies ; we must submit it to the light of reason, and await the judgment of reason. " The world had better never have been." Let us try soberly to imagine its non-existence. Nothing but vacant space, where now is a universe of worlds that circle and shine to each other as stars ; nothing but black darkness ; no sunlight to make the day, no starlight to break or beautify the night ;

The Bed-rock of Pessimism

nothing but death where now is life; no glad, swift-darting fish in the waters of river or sea; no river or sea for them to be glad in; no green earth for flocks to feed on or flocks for the green earth; no fragrant and lovely flowers; no laden bees to hum; no lark that sings as it soars; no man to think great thoughts and to do battle for the true and good; no woman to love and grow beautiful and happy by loving; no child to prattle; no youth to put its eager questions—nothing, nothing, nothing, absolutely nothing; a dismal, dark, vacant infinite, in place of all the wonder that now is; the melodies that fill the air; the lights that are worlds; the peoples, the races, the nations."[1] Which is better, all this or nothing? Let reason judge, reason alone. We can await her verdict without fear. It comes like a mighty chorus in an everlasting "Yes; being is better than no being." Are the slings and arrows of outrageous fortune, the heart ache and the thousand natural shocks that flesh is heir to, the whips and scorns of time, the oppressor's wrong and all the evil that man and Nature are heir to, too big a price to pay for the wonder, the glory, the mystery of creation, too big a cost to pay for life? Let reason answer.

Is there, however, any individual life that had better never have been? Let us think of a profoundly afflicted life, a life held down in weakness, disease and pain, conscious of its great loss, conscious that it will never enter the battle nor the full joy of life, its one fate and lot to suffer. What of that life? It suffers, but praise God! sometimes with a patience and a joy that silence every complaint and shame our whining. It

---

[1] See Fairbairn, "The Philosophy of the Christian Religion," pp. 130f.

Pessimism and Love

suffers, but it opens the fountains of human sympathy and love ; it moves us to compassion ; it compels us to a gentle service ; at times it becomes an inspiration to the strong to do yet more valiantly.

> " A widow—she had only one !
> A puny and decrepit son.
>   But day and night,
> Though fretful oft and weak and small,
> A loving child, he was her all,
>   The widow's mite.
>
> " The widow's mite—ay, so sustained,
> She battled onward nor complained,
>   Though friends were fewer ;
> And while she toiled for daily fare,
> A little crutch upon the stair
>   Was music to her.
>
> " I saw her then ; and now I see
> That, though resigned and cheerful, she
>   Has sorrowed much.
> She has—He gave it tenderly—
> Much faith ; and carefully laid by
>   A little crutch."[1]

That puny and decrepit life was not in vain. If a life, however poor and painful and held under in affliction, can show patience and love, can break our hearts into sympathy, it is well that that life has been, doubly well, if, beside the small opportunities of this world, there are opportunities to come which mortal tongue cannot declare. To be is always better than not to be.

[1] Frederick Lockyer, "London Lyrics."

The Bed-rock of Pessimism

Life is a good and happy concern for most of us. It is so because God is in our life and in our world. With God in our world we can have faith; we can hope, we can dare to love. And it is faith, hope, and love, that are ours through God's presence in the world, that really make the worth, the joy, the happiness of life. With these three in his life a man can never fail to say " O Lord, I thank Thee that I have seen the light."

THE PESSIMIST ON MONEY: THREE CARTOONS

And I saw that all the labour and skill in work is just the result of one man's jealousy of another. This also is vanity and a striving after wind.—CHAP. IV. 4.

And so, better is a handful of quietness than two handfuls of labour and a striving after wind. And I saw yet another vanity beneath the sun. There is one alone by himself, he hath not a second, neither son nor brother hath he. And there is no end to all his toil, and his eyes are not satisfied with riches. "For whom," saith he, "am I toiling and depriving myself of every comfort?" Yea, this is vanity and an evil business indeed.—CHAP. IV. 6—8.

He who loves money will never be satisfied with money, and he who sets his heart on abundance will never have income enough. This also is vanity. As wealth increases, they increase who eat it, and what advantage hath the owner of it, save beholding it with his eyes?
CHAP. V. 10, 11.

There is a sore evil which I have observed beneath the sun: riches retained for their

The Pessimist on Money

owner yet retained to his hurt. The riches are then lost in a bad business and he has got a son, who has nothing in his hand. Even as he came naked from his mother's womb, so shall he return, going back just as he came, and for all his toil taking nothing which he can carry in his hand. And truly, this is a sore evil. Even as he came, so he shall return, and what advantage hath he of his toil? he hath toiled for the wind. Yea, all his days are spent in darkness and in grief, and much vexation and sickness and anger are his.—CHAP. V. 13—17.

There is an evil which I have seen beneath the sun, and it is often very heavy for man to bear: God gives a man riches and wealth and honour, and for himself he lacks not anything which he might desire, but God does not give him power to get any joy of it, but some stranger enjoys it; this is vanity and a sore evil indeed. If a man beget a hundred sons and live many years; yea, however many may be the days of his years, and he hath no real satisfaction in his blessings (yea, though he should be immortal) and have no burial, I say, better than he is the untimely birth; for, as a breath it came, and in darkness it departeth and with darkness is its name covered; yea, it hath not seen the sun nor known it, yet it hath rest more than that.

Pessimism and Love

And peradventure he live a thousand years twicetold and hath not enjoyed his blessings (it is all the same), for are not all going to one place?—CHAP. VI. 1—6.

The pessimist declares in this passage that all work, industry, or activity among men is due to a spirit of rivalry and personal ambition. Ambition is the great human motive. Now ambition is a word of large and vague comprehension, and is an excellent example of what are called " question-begging terms," differing immensely in meaning according to the objects for which one is ambitious. A man may be ambitious to do in all things the will of his Father in Heaven, or to make his life a social service to his fellows, or to develop all his faculties to their highest form and capacity, but it is not ambition of such noble kind that Koheleth speaks of here and declares to be the spring and source of all human activity. The ambition which he has in mind is much rather the personal jealousy, which leads a man to get the better of his fellows, to rise above them and to outstrip them in the matter of possessions. And no doubt this ambition is a great force in human affairs, rising in some men to Napoleonic dimensions, but never, in any dimension, a thing of loveliness, beauty, and good report. And if it is, as Koheleth says, the spring of all industry, labour, trade, and commerce, then all the work that mankind does under the sun is vanity and a striving after wind, and a handful of pleasant and careless idleness is better than two handfuls of labour. For, ambition driving men to industry so that they may outstrip their fellows, will, if satisfied, only lead to pride and arrogancy of heart;

The Pessimist on Money

if defeated, to hate and bitterness of spirit. Ambition of this order is not simply vanity and a striving after wind : it is a positive evil.

But is this ambition, this spirit of rivalry and competition, the great human motive, the one power that drives man forth to his labour ? With some it certainly seems to be so, the sole dynamic of their active life ; with almost all it plays some part, and its presence, in more or less dimension, can be traced in almost every calling, business, or work under the sun, in the pulpit, in the mill, in the office, in the market-place, in the counting-house, causing no doubt the wheels of human activity to revolve a little more quickly, but somehow robbing man's labour of a perfect purity and of a certain natural beauty and grace. But the spirit of competition and rivalry is not the only motive, nor is it altogether incompatible with motives of a nobler order. A man may be impelled to work by the feeling for duty, and of simple obedience to a conscience which says " Thou shalt do this work " ; or he may work in a spirit of service because he feels that his work somehow enriches and blesses his fellows ; or he may work out of a pure love to God, out of a simple desire to please the Highest ; or he may work scarcely knowing why he works, out of simple love of doing and the satisfaction which faithful industry inevitably brings—works because idleness would be misery and a stupid folly. The spirit of ambition is not absolutely incompatible with any one of these nobler, purer, and sweeter motives, with some or all of them combined, though any one or all of them may become so pure and so strong as to give ambition but small room or even no room at all, and then we have a workman whose eye is

Pessimism and Love

single and whose body is full of light. Ambition is a motive, but not the sole motive, in human affairs. If ambition were to be scrapped, the machinery of life would not stand still, and Koheleth, in emphasising ambition, making it the chief motive, slanders the workman and the work that is done beneath the sun.

We have in this passage three cartoons. The first is of a lonely miser, who has neither son nor brother, no kinsman, no friend with whom he can share the rewards of his toil. He goes on unceasingly at his labour and at his saving. " For whom," he asks, " am I working and depriving myself of every comfort ? " He was evidently getting no happiness for himself out of his work and money and nobody else was reaping any advantage. He was simply slaving, making, saving, and it was vanity and a sore business. But what else could he expect out of such self-centred, miserly conduct ? He could scarcely hope that his solitary miserliness would yield a rich happiness, and he really deserves to feel wretched, and it would be a very strange world if he were anything else. His solitariness perhaps is piteous, but with his wealth he could have made many friends, brought happiness to many a poor and anxious home, and received a gratitude that would have made his heart rejoice. The man, however, who saves for saving's sake, gathers his hoard, little or big, for the sake of gathering, who, with no thought of others, loves money, will never in this world, nor, we may believe, in any world, be happy, for, as the pessimist himself says, " He that loveth silver will not be satisfied with silver." All selfish saving is vanity. A man may save, perhaps ought to save, that he may not become a burden upon others ; he may add, perhaps

The Pessimist on Money

ought to add, to the reserve funds of his business that it may weather seasons of hard financial pressure, and that his *employés*, in such seasons, may not suffer unduly ; but saving for saving's sake, the scraping together of a small hoard for the hoard's sake, and denying oneself many of the simple pleasures of life in so doing, or amassing great wealth for the mere satisfaction of possessing some mammoth calf of gold, is vanity, and ought, in a moral world, to be an exceedingly sore business. Who loves money will never be satisfied with money, and who sets his heart on wealth will never have enough, whatever his income. Thank God he will not. Thank God the hoarding, saving, scraping spirit is never satisfied. What kind of men should we be if money could satisfy us ?

The pessimist in this cartoon gives us a picture of a lonely rich man. Here is a picture of another man. He is not rich, but he has sons and brothers and no end of kinsfolk. He earns his money by hard industry, and every penny he makes is earmarked for this one or for that other. He has sons to educate, an invalid daughter for whom he has to find delicate comforts, a poor relative that looks to him for help. Every penny he makes is needed (and more) for the necessities of others. Does he sometimes groan under his heavy burden, at the never-ending calls on his income that leave him no comfort for himself ? Well ; let him look at the picture of the wealthy man without son, without brother, without a second. Would he change places ? Not he. He may grumble at his heavily-taxed pocket with a half-pretence of grumbling, for he knows it is just these continual calls that have kept his heart enlarged, saved him from meanness and

Pessimism and Love

selfishness, and perhaps a miser's fate. They are not always the happiest who have much and little to do with it ; often they are not half so happy as those who have little and much to do with their little.

"As wealth increases, they increase who eat it, and what advantage hath the owner of it, save beholding it with his eyes ? " As of old, so to-day, expenditure increases with income in an almost perfect proportion. Wages become larger, but the difficulty to make ends meet no smaller. From the larger income there are more mouths to feed and more taxes to pay, so what advantage hath the increase save the beholding of it with the eyes—an exercise not of unmixed joy, we can imagine, to the pessimist as he sees it devoured by a growing horde of devourers. But what does the pessimist really want ? He pitifully declares it an evil to be rich and have no son or brother ; he whines none the less when there is wealth and many to share it. Wealth with loneliness is vanity ; wealth with a multitude round about you is the same. What would he really have ? Surely, one of the most natural satisfactions for a man of wealth is that he can provide maintenance and work for others and that he can share his wealth with them. Every increase in the number of those who " eat his riches " is really a fresh opportunity for his own happiness and his own pleasure in his money. One of the richest joys a man gets out of his income is that his children literally " eat " it, are clothed and educated by it, and through it find a larger entrance into life; and the joy is nowise diminished if, in the process, his own private and personal expenditure has to be curtailed. If, as wealth increases, those increase that eat it, a man will not complain

The Pessimist on Money

unless he love gold, but if he love gold he will complain; and complain, too, if he has no son nor brother, if he is lonely and has no one to eat his riches, for money lovers are never satisfied.

The second cartoon gives a picture of a rich man, who by some mischance loses his wealth. He has a son and the son gets no inheritance. The rich man, deprived of his substance, lives out his days in sorrow, and as he came naked into the world naked goes he forth. To lose money by some misfortune is a sore blow. But even if a man does not lose his wealth or part of it by some mischance, he will inevitably lose it, lose it all, for as certain as we brought nothing into this world so certain is it we can carry nothing out. Man loses every penny of his savings at death, and to lose in life some of it is only a partial anticipation of what will certainly happen. And if a man has no other possession but money, the loss of any of it will be a sore blow, and an unspeakable blow when death takes all, to the uttermost farthing. But money is not the only wealth; there is honour, goodness, charity, and the very spirit of Christ—true wealth, indestructible possessions; and with such indestructible possessions, with such true inalienable wealth, a man will not be staggered by any mischance nor fear death, the spoiler of our mortal goods. Let mischance do its worst, let death take all, he will still be rich with riches imperishable.

And as for the poor son without inheritance, he is the real sufferer. Yes; but in ninety-nine cases out of a hundred the suffering is a blessing in disguise.

The third cartoon is a picture of a wealthy man with riches, treasures and honour, with everything his heart

Pessimism and Love

desires. As for sons, he has a hundred. As for years, he is a simple Methuselah. He lacks, however, the enjoyment of his colossal blessings and, through this lack, it were better if he had never been born. What on earth more does he want? Every mortal thing that mortality can possess is his, and yet his life had better never have been. It is a sore travail. The rich man complains when he has no son, complains when he has a hundred; complains when he is rich, and complains when he is made poor. What does he lack? One thing: " Go and sell all that thou hast and give to the poor." Literally, that is what he needs. " Go and sell all that thou hast." Rich, he was a money lover. He must break absolutely with that love, in the only way possible to him, by getting rid of his wealth. We must all, rich or poor, somehow or other, break with that love. And, thank God, when we do, a better love awaits us, even the love of Christ, which leads us into a larger sympathy, a deeper consideration of others and into a greater power of self-denial, in which things alone mortals find their happiness and peace.

THE USES OF ADVERSITY

It is better to go to the house of mourning than to go to the house of feasting.

Forasmuch as that is the end of all men, and the living will lay it to his heart.

Better is grief than laughter,

For when the face is sad, it is well with the heart.

The heart of the wise is in the house of mourning, and the heart of fools is in the house of mirth.—CHAP. VII. 2—4.

It is better to go to a funeral than to go to a wedding, or to some convivial entertainment; it is better to be morose than mirthful; it is better to weep than to laugh, and the wise man will choose the better part, while the fool will choose mirth, gladness, and social delight, and, by his preference, reveal his folly.

This passage almost seems to declare that the chief end of man is to have a sad heart and a gloomy countenance. A miserable soul with a miserable face is a kind of paragon; and the one school for wisdom is the churchyard, while the school for folly is the house of laughter where there is music and dancing.

Of course the day of one's burial may be better (especially for others) than one's marriage-day, but that tragic possibility scarcely gives justification for

Pessimism and Love

raising melancholy into a general counsel of perfection and for giving the palm of wisdom to the gloomy heart ; and, I confess, the first natural impulse is to condemn these words as morbid and as a piece of unhealthy affectation. No one prefers misery to mirth. No one, unless he have a morose, emotionally perverted and even callous heart, would rather go to a funeral than to a wedding. No one thinks that a sour face means a sound heart. All healthy human nature appeals against the judgment that it is better to weep than to laugh. Nor is this natural impulse to condemn melancholy and to appeal against it as an ideal state without high authoritative support. The New Testament condemns the sad heart and the gloomy countenance. " But thou, when thou fastest, anoint thy head and wash thy face ; that thou be not seen of man to fast." Even when thou art in sorrow and life presses hard upon thee, keep up appearances—a strong heart and a happy face. " Rejoice evermore " ; " rejoice, and again I say, rejoice," is the order of the Christian apostle. " The angel of righteousness," says the " Shepherd of Hermas "—the most characteristic religious book of that age, its " Pilgrim's Progress "—" the angel of righteousness is modest and delicate and meek and quiet. Take from thyself grief, for (as Hamlet will one day discover) 'tis the sister of doubt and ill-temper. Grief is more evil than any other spirit of evil, and is most dreadful to the servants of God, and beyond all spirits destroyeth man. For, as when good news is come to one in grief, straightway he forgetteth his former grief, and no longer attendeth to anything except the good news which he hath heard, so do ye also ! having received a renewal

The Uses of Adversity

of your soul through the beholding of these good things. Put on therefore gladness that hath always favour before God, and is acceptable unto Him, and delight thyself in it; for every man that is glad doeth the things that are good, and thinketh good thoughts, despising grief."[1] Natural impulse and Christian commandment and Christian sentiment are at one in giving their favour and their sanction to *L'Allegro* rather than to *Il Penseroso*.

But in spite of natural feeling and its apparent support from Christian commandment and sentiment, reflection leads to the view that there is not a little truth in those melancholy words of Koheleth. Of course it is plain that to go to the house of mirth is, to most of us at least, more congenial than to go to the house of mourning, and to laugh is a more pleasant thing than to weep. But is it not true that some of the most fruitful lessons of life come to us through darkness and disappointment, trial and tears? Ask one who has gone through some severe trial whether he would obliterate the days of darkness, anxiety and loss, or certain other days of his life, when not a cloud was seen in the sky, not a fear troubled or depressed his heart, when all went merry as a marriage-bell—ask him which of those days he could best do without and the answer is fairly certain: " I could easily spare the days of sunshine; they were happy enough and full of pleasantness, but those days of sadness and suffering brought me something more real, something of abiding worth, something deeper and more personal to myself that I would not be without, and that no

[1] Quoted from Walter Pater's "Marius the Epicurean," Vol. II., pp. 115f.

Pessimism and Love

days of mirth and pleasantness could have given me." And that is not the witness of kill-joys, of the sour-visaged and morose-tempered, but of men and women to whom the light is sweet and the sun a pleasant thing to behold and who delight in gladness, mirth and jollity.

Koheleth says it is well to go to the house of mourning which is the house of death, well to face death and its lessons " and the living will lay it to heart." " How without death (and considering it) could man realise the meaning of life ? How feel the immensity, the God-like qualities, the capability of endless gain or loss contained within the terms of his own being ? The picture of man before and after he knew death, in the ' Legend of Jubal,' is true to experience. In the old, soft, sweet days, before men knew Death they lived in gladsome *idlesse;* they played, they sang, they loved, they danced in a life that had no gravity and no greatness ; but when the second death came and men saw that there had come a sleep from which there was no awakening, a new meaning stole into life. . . . Time took a new value ; affection by growing more serious became nobler ; men thought of themselves more worthily and of their deeds more truly, when they saw that a night came when no man could work. Friends and families lived in a tenderer light, when the sun was known to shine but for a season ; earth became lovelier when they thought the place which knew them now would soon know them no more. The limit set to time drove their thoughts out towards Eternity. The idea of the death which was to claim them bade them live in earnest, made them feel that there was something greater than play ; for death had breathed into life the spirit out of which all worthy and heroic deeds do

The Uses of Adversity

come."[1] The human race was taken to the house of death and the experience was good for the race.

And this value of man's greatest sorrow is not borne home to us only when we think of death in relation to the race, and when we see how it affects for good the whole of mankind, its value is revealed out of the experience of the individual. You have been brought to the house of mourning ; you have loved and lost. You shrank from the ordeal, but it came. The darkness and the desolation descended upon you ; your life was plundered of its dearest treasure, and your heart was left empty of everything but grief. Soon, however, you began to say, "I would not have him back"; soon, far sooner than you expected would be the case, you were resigned and more than resigned, giving to the whole tragic experience a deep acquiescence. You may have felt a certain disloyalty to the beloved dead in the acquiescence, and wondered at your complete submission, but this experience is the emergence of the feeling, a perfectly true one, that as it was well for the lost it was also well for you to lose the bodily presence ; well, in ways you cannot fully estimate or completely follow, that your heart was plundered in its love. You felt perhaps that life henceforth must be more serious in its discharge of its responsibilities, for had you not to try and make good here and in time the loss to time and this present world of the life that had been taken ? Did you not feel that it fell to you to continue and carry on all the grace and virtue that was lost, during your longer day ? And did you not feel that the bond of love was at once knit closer and made eternal ? It was well that you were taken to the house of mourning.

[1] Fairbairn, "Philosophy of the Christian Religion," p. 143.

Pessimism and Love

The uses of adversity are accepted by almost all men ; almost all would endorse sentiments like these : " Misfortune has its uses ; for, as our bodily frame would burst asunder if the pressure of the atmosphere were removed, so, if the lives of men were relieved of all need, hardship and severity, if everything they took in hand were successful, they would be so swollen with arrogance that though they might not burst they would present the spectacle of unbridled folly—nay, they would go mad. And I may say further, that a certain amount of care or pain or trouble is necessary for every man at all times. A ship without ballast is unstable and will not go straight." Sentiments like those receive general acceptance. But suffering is not simply an antidote to evils like arrogance and unbridled folly, nor simply a correction to " florid and gaudy prospects and expectations," teaching us " to lower our notions of happiness and enjoyment," and bringing " them down to the reality of things, to what is attainable, to what the frailty of our condition will admit of," it is a positive necessity if such virtues as patience, self-control, endurance, and submission are to exist at all. Half at least of what is called strength of character is cradled and nurtured in the school of suffering. Adversity may seem, " like the toad, ugly and venomous," but it " wears yet a precious jewel in his head."

But difference of opinion may arise over the question of voluntary suffering, of actually going to the house of mourning. To accept suffering when it comes is one thing, to go to it is quite another. Yet how else save by going to suffering, how else but by taking one's self to the house of mourning, in sympathy and with practical help, can the quality of compassion ever grow

The Uses of Adversity

to strength and fulness in the heart ? And compassion, not simply of the impulsive kind, but trained and exercised by going to the house of mourning, to the needy and the distressed, is necessary to our complete humanity. We shall simply be poorer in manhood and in womanhood if we try to avoid the house of sorrow and affliction and go not at times of our own free will and desire. As a simple matter of fact, for the highest and richest life pain and suffering are an absolute necessity. Consider Jesus. Without His sorrows, His Gethsemane, His Cross, He never could have become the perfect Son of God—perfect in obedience and perfect in love. He was made perfect through sufferings. Suffering was the field, and the only field, where His perfection could have been realised. And if we are to approximate to that life it will be on the same field. Sacrifice without pain or suffering is an impossibility, and the life of sacrifice is the highest and richest ; it is the life of love. The world of men and women has so much pain to its hand because the world is built for sacrifice and the life of perfect love. How could we possibly rise to a life which is a filling up of the sufferings of Christ in a world where pain were impossible or reduced to a minimum ? And the highest life, the life of loving sacrifice, is the life of joy, of joy in the suffering and the pain. Paradoxical as it may seem, it is none the less true that pain is in the world that the world's joy may be full. To run away from the house of mourning is to run away from the house of joy. We never know the full joy of life until we suffer in our love and for others' sake.

Are we then to be always seeking pain ? always voluntarily to be bearing suffering ? Are we to make

Pessimism and Love

ourselves everlastingly miserable ? to wear the hair shirt and become morose ascetics ? Far from it. God means His children to rejoice. The impulses of our heart, the words of the New Testament, and Christian feeling declare joy to be the Divine intention for us all. The man who simply tries to make himself miserable defeats the Divine purpose. God says " Rejoice, rejoice," and that His command may receive a full-orbed realisation He has put pain in the world. But to Love alone, pain is the gateway into joy. To selfishness and self-seeking, pain is pain, nothing but pain, a hateful evil. When we suffer for ourselves, for our own sakes, even for the sake of our personal and eternal salvation, we are only miserable ; when we suffer for others, we rejoice with the joy of love itself. Our natural instinct is right when it says " Rejoice," but it is mistaken when it shirks the pain and complains at the suffering as a disturbance of joy ; suffering is the one avenue into the joy of Christ. Christian feeling is right when it says " Rejoice always," but Christian feeling will never realise its own command till it finds in the cross of suffering, in love that involves pain, the eternal well-spring of all joy. " To you," says Paul, " has this grace—this joy—been given not only to believe in Christ, but to suffer for Him."

It is well that we go to the house of mourning, tears and sorrow ; for there, when we go in love for others' sake and service, we touch the perfect life and taste the perfect joy.

THE PESSIMIST ON WOMAN

And more bitter than death have I found woman, for she is a snare; her heart is a net; fetters are her hands. A good man before God shall escape from her, but a sinner shall be captured by her. See! this have I found, saith Koheleth, taking one thing with another, to find out the reckoning that my soul hath ever sought and I have not found. One man among a thousand I have found, but a woman among all these I have not found.

CHAP. VII. 26—28.

This is the judgment of the pessimist on woman. To say the least, it is not a lofty one. There is no chivalrous, ideal, reverent attitude here. Woman, she is more bitter than death; she is a snare; her heart is a net; her arms are chains. Escape from her is a reward of piety and goodness; to be captured by her is a punishment of wickedness. She is the curse of man. So bitter is this judgment that many commentators say that Koheleth is here speaking only of the wicked and abandoned woman who is so realistically described in the seventh chapter of the Book of Proverbs —the woman whose house is the way to hell, a going down to the chambers of death. If that were so, the bitterness becomes intelligible and in part excusable,

Pessimism and Love

especially if the pessimist himself had been a captive to her wiles, though even then it is only fair to remember that, if the woman had sinned, she had been sinned against ; if she had ruined many, she herself had been ruined. But really Koheleth makes no moral distinctions among women in this passage ; it is a pious and charitable interpretation only that makes him do so ; he sweeps all women into his biting, bitter, cynical condemnation, making no difference between good and bad. Woman, she is more bitter than death ; one decent man among a thousand have I found (it is well to notice that the proportion is not great), but never, though I have assiduously looked, have I found one woman worthy of consideration.

Instinctively the question arises, Why this bitterness towards woman ; why this sweeping, unjust, uncompromising condemnation ? No doubt the Oriental treatment of woman had in Koheleth's days penetrated into Jewish circles, and when women are regarded without respect, given an inferior position, treated as the playthings and slaves of men, refused all education in their gilded prisons, regarded with distrust and suspicion, at the best with a kind of amiable contempt, it is no wonder if they become silly and cunning and thoroughly bad. The age when Koheleth lived was certainly not favourable to the growth of gentle and gracious womanhood. But surely there were some good women in Koheleth's day and place, enough to keep living a decent ideal of womanhood, enough to keep any man from this bitter and venomous judgment.

I have sometimes thought that in this passage we have a piece of autobiography. Koheleth is speaking

The Pessimist on Woman

out of some bitter personal experience of his own. He had loved and lost. He had been deceived by some woman, and he sought retaliation in a venomous hatred of all womankind. But, on fair consideration, I fear I must acquit him of ever having been a victim of the grand passion. Koheleth had never loved; he had never lost. He was far too much of an egotist for that. If he had sincerely and passionately and hopelessly loved one woman, he never would have been the bitter pessimist and materialist he was. If he had loved he never would have said " All is vanity and a pursuit after wind," and would never have squirted forth this venom of his upon all womankind ; for it is not the disappointment of love that makes life bitter, it is the disappointment of our selfishness and selfish desires. We want and we do not get, and then become bitter and we hate. We love, and should our love be unrequited, we only love with a love more sacrificially and more self-effacing. Koheleth had never loved.

He was a materialist, a sceptic, a practical atheist, and his judgment upon woman was part and parcel of his creed, the legitimate outcome of his hard and loveless faith. To a materialist, woman is a physical organism naturally weaker than man, with the natural lot of the weak, which is to serve the strong. Woman, in a materialistic world, is simply the slave of the stronger ; she may be petted and spoilt or she may be despised and contemned, but she is a slave all the same. Take any materialist—he does not need to be a scientific or philosophic one, but a man who lives for his own selfish and material ends and who by material force (probably called push or determination) tries to gain them ; he expects everything and everybody weaker than himself to give way to his physical superiority and to satisfy his desires ; everything, woman included, must be his servant, the handmaid of his desires ; and, so long as she performs this function satisfactorily, she may be liked, petted and spoilt, but in all the spoiling, petting and liking there will be a dash of contempt, the contempt which the strong has for the weak. And then the contempt will almost inevitably become hate, for either the woman will cease to be the handmaid of his desires, or else his selfishness will recoil on himself, come home carrying a bitter penalty to his heart, and, with the cowardice common to all selfishness, he will curse, not his own folly, but the woman. A woman has no chance with a materialist, no chance in a materialistic world. Take away God, faith, and love out of the world and you take away at the same time chivalry, reverence, and respect towards womanhood. With the sanctities of religion stand or fall the sanctities of womanhood. We say that women are more religious than men ; no wonder, for religion is their salvation. A materialistic creed means a low ideal of woman ; a spiritual means chivalry and reverence. Koheleth was a materialist—" Woman, she is more bitter than death."

Woman is more bitter than death ; that is the sober and serious judgment of our pessimistic materialist. But sometimes a judgment condemns the judge more than the one who is judged. That is so here. Materialism, not womanhood, is disgraced by this judgment. Contempt for woman is a dirty flag to fly, and he who flies it shows the dirty pirate ship he sails.

This judgment on womanhood is in the Bible, but not of the Bible. It is not the Bible's judgment on woman, not its last and total word on feminism. Far

The Pessimist on Woman

from it. This is not even the judgment of the Old Testament. In the Book of Genesis woman's position is one of subjection to man ; but she is not really inferior to him. She is a helpmeet for him, bone of his bone and flesh of his flesh. She is God-made and God-inspired, even as man is. In patriarchal times the women, Sarah, Rebekah, and Rachel, have their faults ; they are deceitful and jealous, but they are morally no worse than the men with whom side by side they take their place. In the period of the great deliverance from Egypt Miriam is ranked with Moses and Aaron. In the days of the judges Deborah is not only a prophetess, but herself a judge. In the times of the kings, Jezebel in the Northern Kingdom and Athaliah in the Southern are illustrations of the political power and influence that women might wield. The women in religious matters are practically equal with men, accompanying them to the sacred feasts and taking part with them in acts of sacrifice and in the choral service of the temple. Proverbs rises almost to a lyric note in its praise of the virtuous woman (Chap. XXXI.). As a whole the Old Testament honours womanhood and gives to woman a place of dignity and real worth.

But it is when we come to the New Testament that we find womanhood blossoming forth in richest, spiritual beauty. Christ gave to womanhood a new value ; by His chivalrous and courteous conduct not only to good and pure women, but to women who had been wronged, by His free communication of the highest truth to them, by His own gracious and grateful dependence on their help, He gave to the world a new ideal and brought woman to her rightful place. He was so impartial to

Pessimism and Love

men and women with His grace and favour, made them so equal in spiritual privilege, that His apostle could say that in Christ there is neither male nor female. Some of Paul's restrictions on woman's action are a little difficult for us to understand—for instance, his forbidding them to speak at public worship ; but in that word—" in Christ is neither male nor female "—he has stated the great Christian principle which must guide and interpret every word that Paul wrote and every word and opinion that we may express on woman's place and duty in the world. " Neither male nor female in Christ " means that woman, no less than man, can receive all the grace and life that are in Christ ; through her womanhood, with its opportunities and limitations, she can reveal that grace and life, and continue the incarnation of the Eternal Son of God. That is the real glory of womanhood, a glory which woman shares equally with man. In the early Christian Church woman rises into a prominence which she had in no other society of antiquity. She was the equal in spiritual privilege with man, even though she had not the same functions. She does not undertake the same ministerial activities as Paul, but she has the same right and privilege to serve Christ by her woman's powers and opportunities as Paul had by his man's. Through Christ she attained a spiritual freedom not to do anything and everything, least of all to ape masculinities—but to use and consecrate all that was most truly and distinctively womanly in her nature for the highest service, even for Christ and His Kingdom. She can reveal the grace and life of Christ, in a form and beauty impossible to man, and so enlarge and fulfil the revelation of the Son of God.

The Pessimist on Woman

The modern problem of feminism has, to say the least, become a little complex, and to apply the Christian principle to all its ramifications is not altogether easy. But there is man with his natural faculties and opportunities and woman with hers; they are different, but both can serve Christ and be channels of the one Divine Life. There is an absolute spiritual equality which surely dispels all sex rivalry. The man need not cease to be man nor the woman to be woman for that equality to be realised. They can, when Nature and wisdom dictate, unite in the one great service, do the same things; they can, again when Nature and wisdom dictate, separate and do different things, and no violation is done to their real equality. They may share the same office or they may have different offices (and surely Nature says at times they must have), but they still have the one Spirit, the one Service, the one Life. In Christ they are one, equal and the same.

Pessimism in its modern forms, like the ancient, has no high ideal of womanhood. Modern pessimism likes to gloat over the fact that among the intellectual giants of history, the great painters, the musicians, the poets, the thinkers, there are few, very few women. It may be so. Perhaps woman has not yet had her chance on the intellectual fields. She may not have the physical energy, the inexhaustible nervous vitality that excelling greatness in the arts demands, and it is no discredit, if, wanting the force, she could not perform the task. But woman has given an efficient service in other ways, and even pessimism grants that she has one advantage, if advantage it be, over man, and that is in her power to suffer. Power to suffer! What an

Pessimism and Love

advantage ! Capacity for sacrifice, power for the Cross, power to make up that which is lacking in the sufferings of Christ. Power to suffer is greater than power to paint. Romney, the English artist, left his girl wife immediately after he married her, because Sir Joshua Reynolds said that marriage spoilt the artist, and he never saw her again till she returned to him as he lay dying in mental and bodily agony, forgave him, and soothed his last hours. Romney had power to paint ; she had power to suffer. He was an artist in colour ; she an artist in Christ.

The ideal of womanhood as Christ has given it to us is one for man's highest reverence. It may be said that the ideal is ; but what of the actual woman ? Are there no silly, stupid, frivolous and vain women in the world ? Possibly, and possibly their name is legion. But in the New Testament the story is told of a merchant who, of set purpose, went to look for pearls. He found pearls and one of great price. He was a pearl-fisher. Had he gone to gather mud, he possibly would have found mud and been a scavenger. If we look for pearls we shall probably find pearls ; if for mud, our scavenging may be quite successful. If we look with Christ's eyes on womanhood, we shall see the ideal beauty He saw in every woman, even in the plain, the uninteresting and the foolish, a remark which conclusively shows that the reflections in this paper are really meant, not for women, but for men.

IS GOD NEUTRAL?[1]

To all men there is one and the same fate, to the righteous and to the unrighteous, to the clean and to the unclean, to him that offereth a sacrifice and to him that doth not ; as it is with the good, so is it with the sinner, and it is with him who sweareth falsely as with him that honoureth an oath. This is an evil that pervades everything done beneath the sun, that there is one fate to all ; and yea, the heart of the sons of men is full of evil, and madness is in their hearts all their lives, and their end is to go to the dead.—CHAP. IX. 2, 3.

The title of this chapter was " made in Germany." A short time ago a German court-preacher delivered a sermon with that title in Berlin. From the brief notice of the sermon I gather that the court-preacher's argument ran something like this : God is righteous and the ally of the righteous. That was the major premiss. The minor premiss : the Germans are a righteous people and possess a severely virtuous army. The conclusion was then quite simple ; God is not neutral, but the firm ally of Teutonic arms. The argument is perfect in its formal logic, but it adds another proof to the fact that by formal logic you cannot establish the truth or reality of anything.

[1] Written March, 1915.

Pessimism and Love

What is wrong with the argument is the slight material fallacy in the second premiss, which might be truer to fact if the word " severely " were left out, still truer if you left out the words " virtuous " and " righteous," but having done that, there is nothing left. It is unwise at all times to put faith in formal logic, which can be made to prove anything. For instance, by formal logic you can easily prove a thief to be a great benefactor of society. Surplus wealth is an evil of society. A thief relieves society of its injurious surplus wealth. Therefore a thief is a moral benefactor of society. There are many questions that formal logic cannot solve ; the precise value of a burglar is one, the full effect of the light waves that stream through the millions of miles of space from the sun to this planet of ours is another; and, to speak quite reverently, the question of the neutrality or non-neutrality of God is a third.

The pessimist believes in the neutrality of God, not on the basis of formal logic, but on the solid groundwork of fact. He had seen " folly set in great dignity," " servants upon horses and princes walking as servants upon the earth," the poor oppressed and their oppressor prosperous and triumphant, the righteous suffering and the wicked prospering, the same lot falling upon the righteous and the wicked, upon the clean and the unclean, upon him that sacrificeth and upon him that sacrificeth not, upon the good and upon the evil, upon him that sweareth and him that feareth an oath. What did all this show but the simple moral indifference of God, the unconcern of God before moral distinctions— His absolute neutrality ?

In ordinary times, in times of peace and general

Is God Neutral?

prosperity, any healthy-minded man or woman would repudiate the pessimist's conclusion and regard it as a simple piece of morbid and freakish moralism, but to-day I confess that there are facts which seem to give support to the pessimist's belief in the absolute neutrality of God. We are in the thick of the greatest and fiercest war of all history, a war which is to decide most stupendous human issues—the future of civilisation hangs upon it ; and the decision depends—on what ?—on men and munitions. The war is a trial of strength, and its result a question of physical dynamics. Victory will be again, as always, on the side of the big battalions. The strong man will win in his strength, and God's share in the contest is, at the best, only that of a more or less interested spectator. There is a further consideration which seems at the present time to suggest the neutrality of God. Europe has been deluged with blood. The best of its manhood has been slain. Hearts have been plundered of their dearest earthly treasure. Fear sits at countless hearts. And worse than all the sorrow, fear and death that have fallen upon us, is the spate of passionate hate that has swept into the stream of civilisation. Vile deeds have been done in the name of patriotism, and nations have gloried in their shame. And yet we lift up our eyes on high and behold ! the Almighty God spreadeth out the heavens as a curtain and spreadeth them out as a tent to dwell in. We lift up our eyes and behold the stars. He bringeth out their host by number. He calleth them all by names. Not one faileth. In spite of the awful spate of blood and hate God continues His wondrous astronomy in the heavens in absolute peace. He calleth the stars out by name. Not one is lacking.

Pessimism and Love

He is quite undisturbed. Is God neutral and indifferent to all our mundane tragedy and woe ?

We look around, we open our eyes, and unstop our ears and behold ! the promise of spring. The trees are now putting forth shoot and bud. The sound of birds is heard in the morning and in the evening twittering beneath the eaves. Nature is clothing herself in her beautiful garments and rehearsing her joyous notes. The Divine Naturalist pursues His work as usual. Aye ; a million hearts may break, but Nature silences not one note of all her joy. The world moves on its wonted ways. The sun rises and sets. The moon and stars come forth in their glory. Spring heralds her glad approach. All this continues without change and without disturbance, while cruel death and murderous hate strew their agonies and seal the very fountain of human life. God's in His Heaven and in His Nature, but all's wrong with the world. Is He neutral ? A nation's heart may bleed, a little child's may break, and the heavens and the earth are unmoved. Surely their Creator is neutral.

But suppose in a time of national crisis a man is observed to be pursuing his ordinary duties with his ordinary quietness and confidence, it would be scarcely fair from your limited observation of his demeanour to accuse him of indifferentism, of callousness and unpatriotic neutrality. You must know more of the man. He must speak openly. He must reveal himself. You must see his heart and know his character before you judge him and his attitude. Beneath his calm there may be a heart on fire. And so with God ; we must not judge His attitude hastily from dynamics, or from the undisturbed astronomy of the heavens, or

Is God Neutral?

from the unceasing and tireless processes of Nature. It is the real heart of God we need to know, to find an answer to the question, Is God neutral?

There is one word of Jesus which reveals the heart of God and which is very pertinent to the question of the Divine neutrality. "God maketh," says Jesus, "the sun to rise on the evil and on the good, and sendeth rain on the just and the unjust." God's love is universal for all men; it is impartial; it is positive. That is the meaning of the word of Jesus. God loves every nation, people and individual. His benefits are freely offered to all. Nothing can change that love. No sin, national or individual, can destroy it. Man may become unjust and evil, frightful and barbarous, but God still causes His sun to rise upon him and sendeth him rain that quenches the thirst of land and people. God loves the German nation and people with the same love with which He loves the British nation and people. He loves the Emperor William as He loves King George or King Albert of Belgium. God's love, energetic, positive, redeeming, is for all men, always there for the meanest criminal and for the greatest saint. God's greatest gift, the gift of His absolute sacrifice, the gift which is the very expression of His love—that very love itself, His Christ, is there for the evil and the good, for the just and for the unjust. God is the true ally of all (if they only knew it), of the wicked and of the righteous, of all the sons of men without respect of moral person. That is one of the great fundamental principles of the Gospel, and its truth has been abundantly proved in the nineteen centuries of Christian faith.

But there is another principle which we must take

Pessimism and Love

into account if we are to understand how the universal positive love of God works itself out amongst men—this principle that a beneficent power, if we obey it, blesses and helps us ; but the same power, if we disobey it, curses and ruins us. This principle is true of all beneficent powers. It is true with regard to the beneficent power of Nature. "There was a time when the ignorance of man divided all natural forces into two hostile camps. One army of natural forces was fighting against man ; the other army was fighting for his good. The sunshine was his friend, the cruel lightning was his enemy. But what have we learnt as science has brought us more into the soul and heart of Nature ? Is it not this ?—that there is no force of Nature deliberately set to do man harm ; that the most apparently hostile force, if we can understand and obey it, treat it after its own laws and nature, becomes our constant friend and firm ally ? The lightning that once was only hostile and cruel is, now that man understands it, his pitying slave, carrying from one end of the world to the other his tenderest messages. Man says that he rules Nature and she does his work, but the real truth is that she does none of his work, except as he obeys her, docilely studies her ways, and suits himself to her ways."

Nature is a beneficent power. Obey her, and her beneficence is a blessing ; disobey her, and her beneficence becomes a curse. This principle applies to public law and government. These are beneficent powers. They protect life and property ; they give civil security and peace. Through the laws of the land we go about our daily business without fear. But if we disobey them, if we break the laws of our country,

Is God Neutral?

at once they become hostile and punish and afflict us. The principle is true of every beneficent institution—true of education, true of the home, true of the Church. It is supremely true of the love of God. If we obey that love, if we subject ourselves to its influences and become mastered by its spirit, it is our salvation; if we disobey it, refuse to let its authority and influence pervade and guide our life, it is our destruction. Capernaum was exalted to heaven, but that very exaltation (through her disobedience) proved her destruction and thrust her down to hell. And so we may have a nation which God has loved and greatly prospered, to which He has given material wealth, political influence and power, and many of the gifts of civilisation: if that nation is true to the spirit and power of love, that have so enriched her, if she receives her gifts with devout gratitude, and if she is willing and desirous to use them in the service of man, then the love of God and all its beneficence will be true wealth and blessing; but if she becomes arrogant and self-aggrandising, refusing to obey and by obedience to receive the spirit of love that has so generously enriched her, then all that love and its beneficence become her curse. Or we may have a nation settled on its lees; its ideals are dimmed; its temples of the living God are emptied, and its temples of pleasure are crowded. The very race itself is sacrificed on the altar of pleasure and the laughter of little children is silenced. What will all the goodness and love of God prove to that people? Ruin and destruction. But to that nation there comes a call—the call of love, to sacrifice for God's ideals and Kingdom, and in a great act of national repentance her people answer the call, obey its behest and break the god of pleasure into pieces, then the love of God will prove to be life and salvation. God's love is of the one and same moral quality to all nations and individuals, but it depends upon nations and individuals, rests with their obedience or disobedience, whether His love shall bring life or death, salvation or destruction, blessing or curse.

In a war, social or military, between might and right it might be expected that a righteous God would interfere or intervene on the side of right. Non-intervention seems like neutrality and moral indifferentism. But we may well ask whether words like "interfere" and "intervene" are pertinent to the action of One who is omnipresent and the life and sustainer of all men and things. And perhaps still more relevant would be the question whether God would be love, whether He would be performing a loving act if He did interfere or intervene on the side of the righteous. For suppose God did intervene on the side of the righteous whenever they were in a difficult situation, how would the righteous come to regard themselves ? They would come to think of themselves as the special favourites of Heaven, and, whenever a hard task or burden was placed upon them, they would be looking for some special interference of Heaven. They would become the spoilt children of an indulgent Heaven ; they would cease to be true sons of God learning obedience and strength through the burdens and sufferings which they were being called upon to bear. Special interventions for the righteous would turn the righteous into prigs and moral weaklings.

And still further, if God were to interfere by special interpositions, what would those on whose behalf they

Is God Neutral?

were made think of God? They would think of God as their special property. They would lose sight of that word of Jesus that God makes His sun to rise on the just and the unjust, and sendeth forth His rain for the good and the evil. God would become the god of a righteous tribe and not the loving God of the whole world. He would be the monopoly of the few, not the Saviour of all.

To all men there is the same fate, " to the righteous and to the unrighteous, to the clean and to the unclean, to him that offereth a sacrifice and to him that doth not ; as it is with the good so it is with the sinner, and it is with him that sweareth falsely as with him that honoureth an oath." There is one moral world with the same laws for all men, and one God with the same positive unchanging and unchangeable love for all men. God is not neutral, still less is He careless or morally indifferent. God is a beneficent, universal, positive power. Nor can we be neutral. We must either obey that power or disobey it. Obey it, and we are righteous and have the life and love of God. Disobey it, and we are wicked, and lose that life and love. There is one fate or chance or happening to all ; there we agree with the pessimist. That fate or chance is the love of God, *the* beneficent Power. What it shall be to us depends on ourselves, on our obedience or disobedience —there we part company.

THE WORDS OF THE PESSIMIST

The pessimist is a Jew whose faith has suffered shipwreck. He thinks of Nature as under the iron law of necessity, and has come to the conclusion that practically everything is vanity which the Jewish religion has held as reality and truth. Natural, not ethical, law rules everything. There is no living and personal Providence, as the course of nature and the world plainly shews. Man's lot is a continual and vain striving. Pleasure helps nothing, for it rests on a delusion; nor can wisdom give any true satisfaction, for the search for it is resultless. At the best he retains a few thin vestiges of theistic belief.

Vanity of vanities, saith Koheleth, vanity of vanities, the whole world is vanity!

What profit is there to man in all his toil, toiling as he does beneath the sun?

One generation goeth and another cometh,

While the earth remains standing for ever.

And the sun rises and the sun sets,

Going to its place and panting is it to rise there again.

Going unto the south and circling unto the north, circling, circling goes the wind,

And unto its circlings returns the wind ever again.

The Words of the Pessimist

All the torrents go to the sea,
And the sea is not full.
Unto the place where the torrents go,
Thither they go and go.
All things are full of a weariness which no man can declare,
And eye cannot be satisfied with seeing, nor ear filled with hearing.
What has been will be; and what has been done that will be done again.
And there is no new thing under the sun.
Is there a thing of which it is said, "Lo, this indeed is new"?
It hath existed already in the ages which were before us.
There is no remembrance of our forbears.
Nor will there be any remembrance of those who are yet to be, amongst later generations.

I, Koheleth, was king over Israel in Jerusalem.
And I gave my heart to search out and investigate by wisdom all that is done beneath the heavens: it is an evil business God hath given to the sons of men to be busied with.
I have seen all the works which are done beneath the sun; and, behold the whole is vanity and a striving after wind.

> The crooked cannot be made straight,
> And what is lacking cannot be counted.

Pessimism and Love

I spake with my heart saying, "As for me! lo, I have become great and increased wisdom, above all that were before me over Jerusalem, and my heart hath experienced in abundance wisdom and knowledge."

And I gave my heart to know wisdom, and to know madness and folly. I have experienced that this also is a striving after wind. For in much wisdom is much vexation, and he that increaseth knowledge increaseth pain.

And I said in mine heart, "Come now, I will try thee with mirth, and do thou try pleasure." And lo! even this is vanity. Of laughter I said, "It is mad." And of mirth, "What is the good of it?" I resolved with myself, to cheer my flesh with wine (yet I continued to behave myself wisely) and to lay hold of folly, until I should see, where is this pleasure for the sons of men, which they have beneath the heavens all their life long. I did great things. I built houses for myself; I planted vineyards for myself. I laid out for myself gardens and parks, and planted in them all kinds of fruit trees. I made for myself pools of water, from which to water a wood with young trees. I bought menservants and maid-servants, and servants born in the house were mine; yea, cattle-steadings and sheep-runs were mine in abundance. I had

The Words of the Pessimist

more than all that were before me in Jerusalem. I gathered for myself silver and gold, and the choice treasures of the kings and the provinces. I got for myself men-singers and women-singers, and the delights of the sons of men. . . . Yea, I became great and increased above all that were before me in Jerusalem, yet my wisdom remained by my side. And all that mine eyes desired I withheld not from them, and I kept not my heart from any delight, for my heart was delighting in all my labour, and that was my portion from all my labour. And I turned to consider all my works which my hands had made, and to the labour which I had put forth in my work, and lo ! the whole is vanity and a pursuit after wind and there is no profit beneath the sun. For what will a man do that cometh after the king ? That which hath been already done.

And I turned to try wisdom and madness and folly, and my conclusion is that the same fate happeneth to them all. Then I said to myself, " A fate similar to that of the fool will come to me, why then have I become so exceptionally wise ? " And I said in mine heart, " Yea, this is vanity." For the wise as little as the fool is remembered for ever, and in days to come every one is forgotten ; and how should the wise

Pessimism and Love

man die like the fool? Then I hated life, for hard and evil upon me is the work which is done beneath the sun, for all is vanity and a striving after wind; and I hated all my toil in which I toiled beneath the sun, for I shall leave all its fruits to the man who shall come after me, and who knoweth whether he will be a wise man or a fool? And yet he will have power over all the results of my toil and wisdom which I had beneath the sun. Yea, this is vanity.

Every thing has its appointed day, and every business beneath the heavens has its time.
> There is a time to be born,
>> And a time to die.
> There is a time to plant,
>> And a time to uproot.
> There is a time to wound,
>> And a time to bind the wounded.
> There is a time to break down,
>> And a time to build up.
> There is a time to weep,
>> And a time to laugh.
> There is a time to lament,
>> And a time to dance.
> There is a time to cast stones away,
>> And a time to gather stones.
> There is a time to embrace,
>> And a time to refrain from embracing.

The Words of the Pessimist

There is a time to seek,
   And a time to lose.
There is a time to keep,
   And a time to cast away.
There is a time to rend,
   And a time to sew together.
There is a time to be silent,
   And a time to speak.
There is a time to love,
   And a time to hate.
There is a time of war,
   And a time of peace.

What benefit hath the worker for all his toil?

I have seen the work which God hath given to the sons of men for their busy occupation [it is all vanity].

What happened in the past, it had already happened at a still earlier date, and what will happen in the future has already happened in the past, for God seeketh (ever and again) that which hath disappeared.

And, further, I have perceived beneath the sun, that in the place of judgment there is iniquity, and in the place of righteousness there is iniquity.

And I said in mine heart, " This is because of

Pessimism and Love

the sons of men, to prove them hath God done it, and that they may see that they are beasts, simply beasts." For mere chance are the sons of men and chance are the beasts; there is the same chance (or fate) to them both: as one dieth so dieth the other; and one spirit is to all, and the advantage of man over the beasts is nothing, for the whole is vanity. All go to one place; all are from the dust, and all return to the dust. Who knoweth the spirit of the sons of men, whether it goeth upward and the spirit of the beasts whether it goeth downward to the earth?

And again I considered all the oppressions which happen beneath the sun; and see! what is there but the tears of the oppressed? and they have no comforter. On the side of the oppressors there is power, but the oppressed have no comforter. And I congratulated the dead, who are already dead, rather than the living, who are still alive. And more than both of them is to be congratulated he who hath not yet been and hath not seen the evil work that is done beneath the sun.

And I saw that all the labour and skill in work is just the result of one man's jealousy of another. This also is vanity and a striving

The Words of the Pessimist

after wind. And so, better is a handful of quietness than two handfuls of labour and a striving after wind.

And I saw yet another vanity beneath the sun. There is one alone by himself: he hath not a second; neither son nor brother hath he. And there is no end to all his toil, and his eyes are not satisfied with riches. "For whom," saith he, "am I toiling and depriving myself of every comfort?" Yea, this is vanity, and an evil business indeed.

Better is a youth who is poor but wise than a king who is old and foolish and who is no longer capable of receiving admonition. For out of prison did the youth succeed to the throne, although he had been poor under the rule of the old king. And I saw that all the living that walk beneath the sun were on the side of the youth who was to take the place of the king. There was no end to all the people, to all whom he was to lead, and yet the later generations did not delight in him. Yea, this also is vanity and a striving after wind.

He who loves money will never be satisfied with money, and he who sets his heart on abundance will never have income enough. This also is vanity. As wealth increases they

Pessimism and Love

increase who eat it ; and what advantage hath the owner of it save beholding it with his eyes ? This is a sore evil, which I have observed beneath the sun—riches retained for their owner yet retained to his hurt. The riches are then lost in a bad business, and he has got a son who has nothing in his hand. Even as he came naked from his mother's womb, so shall he return, going back just as he came, and, for all his toil, taking nothing which he can carry in his hand. And truly, this is a sore evil. Even as he came, so he shall return, and what advantage hath he of his toil ? he hath toiled for the wind.

Yea, all his days are spent in darkness and in grief, and much vexation and sickness and anger are his.

There is an evil which I have seen beneath the sun, and it is often very heavy for man to bear—God gives a man riches and wealth and honour, and for himself he lacks not anything which he might desire ; but God does not give him power to get any joy of it, but some stranger enjoys it ; this is vanity and a sore evil indeed. If a man beget a hundred sons and live many years, and however many may be the days of his years, and he hath no real satisfaction in his blessings, yea (though he should be immortal) and have no

The Words of the Pessimist

burial, I say, better than he is the untimely birth ; for, as a breath it came, and in darkness it departeth and with darkness is its name covered ; yea, it hath no knowledge or joy of the sun ; it hath rest while he hath it not. And peradventure he live a thousand years twicetold and hath not enjoyed his blessings (it is all the same), for are not all going to one place ?

All the toil of man is for his mouth, and yet his appetite will not be satisfied.

Better is the day of death than the day of one's birth.
Better is it to go to the house of mourning than to go to the house of feasting, forasmuch as that is the end of all men, and the living will lay it to his heart.
Better is grief than laughter, for when the face is sad it is well with the heart.
The heart of the wise is in the house of mourning, and the heart of fools is in the house of mirth.

These two things have I noted in the days of my vanity—a righteous man perishing despite his righteousness and a wicked man prolonging his days despite his iniquity.

Pessimism and Love

And more bitter than death have I found woman, for she is a snare; her heart is a net; fetters are her hands. A good man before God shall escape from her, but a sinner shall be captured by her. See! this have I found, saith Koheleth, taking one thing with another, to find out the reckoning that my soul hath ever sought, and I have not found. One man among a thousand have I found, but a woman among all these I have not found.

All this have I seen, while I gave my attention to every work which is done beneath the sun—a time when one man lords it over another man to his own hurt. And afterwards I saw the wicked buried, and they that had done right went away from the holy place and were forgotten in the city: this also is vanity.

There is a vanity which is allowed upon the earth—there are righteous men who are stricken as though their works were wicked, and there are evil men who fare as though their works were righteous; yea, this is vanity.

So often I gave my attention to know wisdom and to understand the business which is done upon the earth (for verily neither by day nor by

The Words of the Pessimist

night does one see sleep in his eyes), that I saw the whole plan of God, which is, that man cannot find out the plan which is being worked out beneath the sun, while man toils away to seek it, but does not find it ; yea, even if the wise man resolve to know it, he cannot find it out.

To all men there is one and the same fate, to the righteous and to the unrighteous, to the clean and to the unclean, to him that offereth a sacrifice and to him that doth not ; as it is with the good, so it is with the sinner, and it is with him who sweareth falsely as with him that honoureth an oath. This is an evil that pervades everything done beneath the sun, that there is one fate to all, and, verily, the heart of the sons of man is full of evil, and madness is in their hearts all their lives, and their end is to go to the dead.

For the living know that they shall die, but the dead know nothing, and they get no more wages, for their very memory is forgotten. Yea their love and their hate, yea their envy, is already perished and they have no further lot for ever in all that is done beneath the sun.

There is an evil which I have noticed beneath

Pessimism and Love

the sun, a blunder as it were for which the ruler is responsible—folly is often set in high places, while the rich sit in humble. I have seen servants upon horses and princes walking like servants upon the earth.

II. THE HEDONIST

II. THE HEDONIST

EPICURUS IN THE OLD TESTAMENT

AND I saw that there is nothing better than that man should rejoice in his works, for that is his portion, for who can lead him to find out that which shall be after him?—CHAP. III. 22.

Lo, this is what I have seen as a good which is beautiful—to eat and to drink, and to see fruit from the toil with which a man toils beneath the sun all the days of his life, which God hath given him, for that is his lot. Further, if God gives to any man riches and wealth and power to enjoy their use, and to take them as his portion, and to rejoice in his labour—well; this *is* the (best) gift of God: for (in such case) a man does not trouble himself about the days of his life (that they are few), for God keeps him occupied with the joy of his heart.

CHAP. V. 18—20.

In the day of prosperity be of good spirits, and in the day of adversity consider; this also even as the other hath God made, because man after his death will have no further experience.

Pessimism and Love

Do not be righteous over much and do not play the wise man to excess; why shouldest thou ruin thyself?—CHAP. VII. 14, 16.

And I commended mirth because there is nothing better beneath the sun for a man than to eat and drink and be merry, and that it may attend him in his toil during the days of his life which God hath given him beneath the sun.—CHAP. VIII. 15.

For only he who is joined to the company of the living hath yet anything to hope for; for, as the proverb goes, a living dog is better than a dead lion.—CHAP. IX. 4.

Go, eat thy bread with joy and drink with a good heart thy wine, for already hath God accepted thy works.—CHAP. IX. 7.

Always let thy garments be white, and oil upon thy head let it not be lacking. Enjoy life with the wife whom thou hast loved all the days of thy passing existence which hath been given thee under the sun, for that is thy portion in life and in thy labour wherein thou labourest beneath the sun. Whatsoever thy hand findeth to do with thy strength, do it; for there is no work or reckoning or knowledge or wisdom in Sheol, whither thou art going. For man also knoweth not his time: even as the fishes that are taken in an evil net and as birds that are caught

Epicurus in the Old Testament

in the snare, so are the sons of men entrapped in an evil time as it falleth suddenly upon them.
CHAP. IX. 8, 9, 10, 12.

For amusement, men prepare a banquet and wine that giveth joy to life, and money is good for everything.—CHAP. X. 19.

Sweet is the light and pleasant is it for the eyes to behold the sun; for if man lives many years, in all of them let him rejoice, remembering that the days of darkness will be many: everything which cometh is vanity. Rejoice, O youth, in thy youth, and let thy heart cheer thee in the days of thy youth, and walk in the ways of thy desire and follow the enticements of thine eyes. And remove sorrow from thy heart and put away evil from thy flesh, for youth and the morning passeth as a vapour. (Rejoice, rejoice) while the evil days come not nor the years draw nigh when thou shalt say I have no pleasure in them, and while the sun be not darkened or the moon or the stars, and the clouds return after the rain. In the day when the defences of the house tremble, and the strong men bow themselves and the few grinders that are, cease to grind, and those that look out of the lattice be darkened, and the doors are shut on the street when the sound of the mill is still, and one riseth at the sound of the bird, and

Pessimism and Love

all the daughters of song are brought low. Yea, of that which is high they are afraid and of the terrors in the way, and the almond tree wears blossom and the caperberry is made ineffectual, for man goeth to his everlasting house and the mourners gather round the street. Until the silver cord is snapped and the golden bowl is crushed and the pitcher is broken by the spring, and the wheel is shattered into the cistern and the dust returns to earth where it was.
CHAPS. XI. 7, 8, 10 ; XII. 1*b*—7*a*.

This is epicureanism or hedonism. But this must be said with qualifications. The physical conception of the world which Epicurus derived from Democritus, and which explains the origin of created things by atoms falling through space slightly off the perpendicular line, is not here, nor is the epicurean theory of knowledge which accounted for experience through the processes of memory, perception, and anticipation. We have in these Biblical epicurean passages no theory of knowledge or of creation. We have simply a *modus vivendi*, a manner of life, commended and extolled. That is the first qualification. The second is that this Biblical epicureanism is not sensualism. Epicureanism is not necessarily debauchery. " Let us eat, drink and be merry, for to-morrow we die," is usually regarded as the alpha and omega of the epicurean catechism ; but, as Mr. Walter Pater has said, it " is a proposal the real import of which differs immensely, according to the natural taste and the acquired judgment of the guests who sit at table." The proposal may lead one

Epicurus in the Old Testament

to libertinism ; it may lead another to the simple life. And it may be said, by the way, that Epicurus himself was inclined to the simple life. "For myself," he wrote to a friend, "I can be pleased with bread and water; yet send me a little cheese, that when I want to be extravagant I may be"; and he boasted that while Metrodorus had reduced his expenditure to sixpence a day, his own was considerably less.

Epicureanism, in popular language, describes a life or system of living that makes happiness or pleasure the end or goal of existence. The end may be perhaps realised in the simple life, or under the hood of a monk, or by making and spending money, and keeping the ten commandments all the time ; but happiness in some mode or other is the end of epicureanism, and it is because the author of these words counsels happiness, pleasure, and enjoyment that we can call him an epicurean or hedonist. Some scholars have tried to trace historical connections between this epicureanism and the Greek epicureanism, and usually derive the Hebrew from the Greek, but such efforts are futile ; nor is it necessary to account for this Hebrew epicureanism by Greek influence. The origin of epicureanism is not in Epicurus, but in human nature itself. A Jew could be an epicurean as easily as a Greek, and we have before us the epicurean *modus vivendi* of an anonymous Hebrew writer whom we name the Hedonist, or Epicurus the Jew.

As epicureanism may take various forms and disguises, for in the matter of pleasure one man's meat may be another man's poison, we have to consider any epicurean philosophy or *modus vivendi* on its own merits, and let us be quite frank and say that in

Pessimism and Love

Epicurus the Jew and in his solution of life there is much that is attractive and morally praiseworthy. Life is to him a pleasant institution. " Sweet is the light, and pleasant is it for the eyes to behold the sun." He has no ungrateful grudge against man or God. He does not go about snarling and barking and gnashing his teeth at the heels of Providence. And he has evidently attained to a fair degree of happiness, which may be taken as proof that he had in his nature a good dash of wholesome moral goodness. A grateful gladness, a simple delight in the warmth and brightness of the sun is no poor testimonial to the essential wholesomeness of a man's nature and life. The " Shepherd of Hermas," which was the " Pilgrim's Progress " of the second Christian century, says : " Put on gladness that hath always favour before God and is acceptable to Him, and delight thyself in it ; for every man that is glad doeth the things that are good, and thinketh good thoughts, despising grief." We may presume that it was this glad, grateful, and genial temper which the epicurean shows that made M. Renan pronounce the Book of Ecclesiastes " charmant, le seul livre aimable qui ait été composé par un Juif." And certainly we may say that no *modus vivendi* or philosophy of life can be considered satisfactory which does not ensure a certain amount of happiness, and no man can be said to have found a practical solution of existence who cannot truthfully declare, in spite of all pessimists and in face of the many ills of life, " Truly the light is sweet." Happiness may not be the end of existence, but it is the sign of a *mens sana* and the condition of all effective goodness. After all, misery is no sign of piety or exceptional virtue.

Epicurus in the Old Testament

And, further, this Jewish epicurean gives excellent advice when he says (according to the punctuation of the Massorites), "whatever thy hand findeth to do with strength, do it." Attention to that word alone might have saved many a human failure. There are a few people who can do all things with strength, but their number is strictly limited ; to a few elect souls every avenue of human activity seems to lie open and every one leads to distinction ; to the vast majority, including even those that may be reckoned gifted and people of talent, the only possibility is to do one or two things decently well. And the problem for most of us is just to discover what we can do with moderate success and serviceableness, a problem that is not always easily and quickly solved. The difficulty, I imagine, is due to our belief that we are born specialists in some subject or other, which, in a few cases, is quite true ; but the vast majority of us are not born specialists—we are born, and still more we have been educated, for general practice. General practice is our *forte*. Well, let us go in for general practice ; let us take the results of the specialist and make them general to the community, and we are then not altogether useless in the world : in a word, let us specialise in general practice. After all, great specialists are only occasionally wanted and consulted ; general practitioners have always an opportunity and a demand.

The mistake, I imagine, that some of us make is that we think that the task which our hand can do with strength requires a great deal of search, and in the search for it, we waste a good deal of useless energy and put forth many futile attempts, and then in disappointment, thinking we are not greatly good for anything,

Pessimism and Love

we return home to find that the thing we have been looking for—the task we can do really well—has been waiting in patience for us at our own fireside, or certainly not very far away from our own door. A man certainly ought to do what he is best fitted for; a round peg in a square hole causes a double discomfort. But usually the round peg has put himself to a vast amount of inconvenience to find the square hole: he has got there of himself, for the forces of Nature and of society do not like misfits; they love and ever seek correspondences and harmonies, the fitting and appropriate union, and if round pegs would only be humble and trust Nature and society, Nature and society would find the fitting sphere. After all, for most of us the problem is not to look with all our strength for something to do, but to do with all our strength the task which Nature, society, and God, taking counsel together, have found for us.

Our hedonist is of service if only for his counsels to happiness and mirth and intensity of living, and we do not wish to withhold from him his moral due. But it is impossible to prevent misgiving and doubt arising as to the worth of his creed as a whole. On his own confession his creed is a creed for youth. It is a creed which only youth can put into practice. The evil days will come when the mirth which he counsels will be no longer possible. Old age, which is described in allegorical and euphemistic language (xii. 1b—7a), will come and epicureanism, even of the most tempered and moderate order, will be no longer possible. The only possible satisfaction and joy that old age can have will be, to look back upon the days of mirth and pleasantness. But will the retrospect give joy and satisfaction?

Epicurus in the Old Testament

" Forty years on, growing older and older,
  Shorter in wind as in memory strong,
Feeble of foot, and rheumatic of shoulder,
  What will it help you that *once* you were strong?"

What will it help us in the evil days that once the days were pleasant and brimful of joy? And alas! most of us are hoping for these evil days of age. On our epicurean's creed we should pray the gods to love us and to slay us at the noon day of our life.

And, further, the epicurean's creed has another defect. It is not universal. It excludes by its very conditions certain estimable people, to wit those who pay little or no income tax and teetotallers, both of whom are worthy of consideration, the latter especially if only on account of their voluntary self-denial. Wine that giveth joy to life and money that is good for everything are, according to the hedonist, both requisite for the attainment of happiness. What, then, of the man who cannot afford for his pocket's sake or for his brother's sake to lay down his *magnums?* He is condemned to an inferior blessedness, which, to say the least, seems to be scarcely a fair and equitable social arrangement.

A third defect is the discouragement which the creed gives to all enthusiasm. "Do not be righteous over much and do not play the wise man to excess; why shouldest thou ruin thyself?" This may be most necessary reproof to the self-righteous Pharisee and to the conceited intellectual, but as a piece of general advice it savours of the cynicism that brings death to all serious striving and effort, and seems scarcely consistent with the intensity involved in the advice to do whatever our

Pessimism and Love

hand findeth to do with strength. Perhaps the hedonist himself was not consistent. He was intense where intensity led to immediate happiness, but in righteousness and knowledge where intensity meant pain and loss of pleasure, he was a moderate. And the great defect of all moderatism is that it is unequal to the demands and the whole battle of life. Epicureanism, in its best form, is moderatism; it has no place for moral heroism and self-sacrifice by which the victories of life and its real treasures are gained, and in times of great moment, personal and national, it has to be driven off the stage. At this present hour[1] we Britons, at least, dare not dally with Epicurus.

The question arises, How and wherefore does Epicurus find a place in Holy Writ? Well; there are good things, as has already been said, in Epicurus; he does remind us that the light is sweet and counsels us, when we feel spite and grudge against life, to be thankful that we are alive, for, as the proverb has it, " a living dog is better than a dead lion." But the Bible is not only God's Book, but man's, and if Epicurus had been left out of the Bible, a part of man's humanity would have been omitted, for in our human pantheon among the gods many, there is the little laughing, attractive deity, who genially invites us all to take our ease and pleasure ourselves as the days slip past.

One thing is certain. Epicurus is not here in Holy Writ because he is perfect and speaks the final word on life. He is here through the broad-minded charity and intellectual fairness of the Bible, which admits all the spirits that men may try them and test their words.

To return and in conclusion. There is no theory of

[1] March, 1915. During the great world war.

Epicurus in the Old Testament

pleasure. We cannot define it, nor can we describe it, with a description that includes its infinite varieties. It has its place in life. It is not the end of life, nor the motive of living. It is the garden where we may rest of an evening and enjoy, simply enjoy, the beauty of colour and the quiet glory of life ; it is the music which turns our step to quicker tread ; above all, it is God's forcible way of calling us miserable liars when we sing

" Earth is a desert drear ;
Heaven is our home."

III. THE PIETIST

III. THE PIETIST

GOOD AND EVIL IN THE PIETIST

YET this power to enjoy, according to my experience, comes from the hand of God, for who can eat or even taste anything apart from Him? For to the man who pleases Him He gives wisdom and knowledge and joy, but to the sinner He gives trouble, letting him gather and heap up, but only in the end to give all to him who is well-pleasing to God.
CHAP. II. 24*b*—26.

Everything hath God made beautiful in its time: yea, the future hath God set in man's heart, so that he cannot interpret the work which God hath made from the beginning unto the end. A man eats and drinks and is prosperous in his labour, but that, in every case, is a gift from God. I have recognised that everything which God doeth shall be for ever, nothing can be added to it and nothing taken from it. And God hath so acted that men may fear before Him.—CHAP. III. 11, 13, 14.

I said in mine heart, God shall judge the righteous and the wicked, for there is a time for every purpose and every work.—CHAP. III. 17.

Pessimism and Love

Guard thy foot when thou goest to the house of God. To draw near to hear is better than to offer the sacrifice of fools, for they are utterly ignorant save to do evil.

Do not rush to thy lips, and let not thine heart be in a hurry to utter a word before God, for God is in the heavens and thou art upon the earth ; therefore let thy words be few. When thou vowest a vow to God, be not slack in fulfilling it, for there is no pleasure to Him in fools. When thou makest a vow, fulfil it. Better not to vow, than to vow and not fulfil. Suffer not thy mouth to lead thee into sin, and say not before the priest, that it was an inadvertence ; wherefore should God be angry with thy word and destroy the work of thy hands? Fear thou God ! If thou seest the oppression of the poor and the wresting of judgment and justice in a province, do not be astonished about the matter, for every high official is guarding his own interests before another, and the highest official more than them all.[1]

CHAP. V. 1, 2, 4, 5, 6, 7b, 8.

Whatever exists its name hath been called,[2] and it is known how it will be with man, and

---

[1] The usual translation is, But the Highest, that is, God is over all. But this, while it accords with the thought of the Pietist, requires that one Hebrew word must be taken in two very different senses in the same verse.

[2] " Its name hath been called "—*i.e.*, its nature is fixed.

Good and Evil in the Pietist

he cannot contend with him that is mightier than himself. For though there be many words, they only increase the vanity of existence; what profit are they to man? For who knoweth what is good for man in life during the number of the days of his life, which he spendeth as a shadow? for who can declare to man what shall be after him beneath the sun?

CHAP. VI. 10—12.

Consider the work of God, for who can make straight what He hath made crooked?

CHAP. VII. 13.

Do not be wicked over much and do not be a fool; why shouldest thou die before thy time?

CHAP. VII. 17.

All this have I tried by wisdom; I said, "I will become wise," but that is far from me. Whatever exists, far off is the meaning of it—deep, very deep, who shall interpret it? I turned my soul to know, to search out and seek wisdom and the account of things, and to know that wickedness is stupidity and folly (moral) is madness.—CHAP. VII. 23—25.

Lo, this alone have I found, that God made man upright but they have found out many devices.—CHAP. VII. 29.

As for me, I say, Observe the king's word, but in the matter of an oath to God be not disturbed, but go from the king's presence, and

Pessimism and Love

continue not in an evil thing, for everything which he pleaseth he doeth. For the word of the king hath power, and who can say, "What doest thou?" He that keepeth God's command shall not know an evil thing, and the heart of the wise will think of time and judgment. For to everything there is a time and judgment, for the evil of man is heavy upon him. For one knoweth not what shall be and how it can be; who can tell him? No man hath power over the wind to restrain the wind, and no man hath power over the day of his death, and there is no discharge in the war, and evil shall not deliver its lords.—CHAP. VIII. 2—8.

Because the decree against an evil work is not executed speedily, therefore the heart of the sons of men is full of the desire to do evil. Though a sinner may do evil for long, and he tarry in his anger, yet I know that it shall be good to those that fear God, yea to those who have fear in His presence.

But it shall not be well with the wicked, and he shall not prolong his days as the declining shadow, for he hath no fear in the presence of God.—CHAP. VIII. 11—13.

Yea, all this have I laid to heart, and have set my heart to search out all this, that the righteous and the wise and their works are

Good and Evil in the Pietist

in the hand of God, with their love and with their hate. . . .[1]—CHAP. IX. 1.

As thou dost not know the way of the wind, nor how the bones form in the womb of her who is with child, so thou dost not know the work of God, who doeth all things.—CHAP. XI. 5.

And know that for all those things (this careless delight and pleasure) God will bring thee into judgment.—CHAP. XI. 9b.

And remember thy Creator in the days of thy youth.—CHAP. XII. 1a.

And the spirit shall return unto God who gave it.—CHAP. XII. 7b.

The pessimist could hardly escape the charge of holding immoral and irreligious opinions. He denies the value of all human endeavour ; he obliterates moral distinctions ; he doubts the righteous government of the world. Such heresy could scarcely pass without protest on the part of orthodoxy, which in the Book of Ecclesiastes finds a defender of the faith against pessimism and epicureanism in one who has been called " a zealot hostile to the book," and the Chasîd (the Chasidim in the Maccabbean age formed a pious and orthodox party who opposed the Hellenisation of Judæa). For the purposes of exposition we call him the Pietist.

Against the view of the pessimist that all human effort is in vain the pietist asserts that this is only so in the case of the sinner ; to the righteous God gives

[1] The meaning of the latter half of the verse is impossible to fix with certainty.

wisdom and knowledge and joy. He depicts the sinner as heaping up and gathering for a season, but only, in the end, to hand over all his gathered wealth to the righteous. Sinners fail and find all to be vanity; the righteous gloriously succeed (ii. 26). As against the pessimistic obliteration of moral distinctions (iii. 19; viii. 14; ix. 2) the pietist asserts that the God-fearing man is protected (vii. 18*b*) and is successful, while the sinner will not escape judgment nor an early death (viii. 12, 13). The pessimist denies the righteous government of the world, but the pietist holds that it will be asserted in a judgment, which, though it may be delayed, will surely come for the justification of the righteous and for the downfall of the wicked. In opposition to the materialism which reduces man and beast to the same level, the pietist holds that the spirit —the breath of man—returns to God who gave it. The pietist also reminds the epicurean or hedonist that his eating and drinking and pleasure in life is a gift of God, and warns him that for all careless enjoyment he will be called to judgment.

Whether the defence of the faith or apology for orthodox religion which the pietist made was successful in counteracting the heretical views of pessimism and epicureanism, we cannot say. But we may presume that the defence had one good result—it helped to secure canonicity for the Book of Ecclesiastes. Without the orthodox reflections in the book, the Jewish scholars would have been in sore straits to know what to do with it, and I fear that, in spite of the fictitious Solomonic authorship, would have been forced to put Koheleth and his epicurean companion on the Index. The orthodoxy of the pietist, we may well suppose, did

Good and Evil in the Pietist

its share in securing for the book canonicity—a place in the sacred library of the Scriptures. Of course the book might have remained uncanonical and yet been preserved for us; but canonicity made its preservation certain, and so, whatever we may think of the pietist and his religious views, we owe him our thanks for the part he played in making sure the preservation of a book whose interest is unfailing.

If one were to seek for a modern term to designate broadly the theology of the pietist, there can be no doubt it would be Calvinist. He is Calvinist in creed and in temper. "Whatever exists," he says, "its name hath been called," that is, its nature is fixed; "and, it is known beforehand how it will be with man," what man's nature and experience will be; and "man cannot contend with Him that is mightier than himself." And again he says: "I have recognised that everything which God doeth, it shall be for ever; nothing can be added to it and nothing taken from it." God's sovereignty is absolute over everything in the world. God hath foreknown man's life and hath fixed all its conditions, so that nothing can be changed. Whatever is, is right, for God hath done it.

This creed brings the pietist to a spirit of deepest submission. The mysterious and hard facts of life, which had made the pessimist break out into bitter complaint against the righteous government of the world, only bring from the pietist words of resignation. For instance, when the pessimist declares that man's experiences are all fixed in an unalterable order—that there is a time to be born and a time to die, a time to weep and a time to laugh, a time to make war and a time to be at peace—and from this fixedness of all

Pessimism and Love

experience feels the utter hopelessness of all human effort, the pietist, on his part, accepts the fixed order as a ground for simple submission. God hath done it, fixed unalterably all human experiences, "*that men may fear Him.*" In face of the order of existence the pessimist is hopeless ; the pietist is resigned, drawing consolation from the beauty which the order everywhere reveals. God hath made everything beautiful in its time.

We have then the two moods, complete despair and complete submission, presented to us, moods closely akin to one another, and sometimes not easily distinguishable ; but the preference must be given to the pietist, for he does not complain out of a bitter heart. Submission is nobler than despair. We can imagine two men upon whom some mysterious, hard, and crushing fate has fallen. The one becomes bitterly hopeless and rebellious ; the other, crushed and broken, submits without complaint and bitterness to the dread necessity. Of the two the latter would command for his mental attitude, I imagine, more moral approval than the former. The difference of attitude may be due to difference in temperament. But in the cases before us there is more than temperament to account for the difference. Of the thirty-nine times that the name of God is mentioned in Ecclesiastes, three-fourths are in the speech of the pietist. God was more to him than to the pessimist. The order of life's experiences might be fixed, but to the pietist it was God's order, a fact which saved him from pessimistic despair to religious submission. But the two moods are closely related, and sometimes so like one another that submission has little or no moral superiority. In some crises resignation may be the only attitude and be far nobler than

Good and Evil in the Pietist

despair, but it is not an ideal mood for all the experiences of life, which calls not only for passive submission, but for passionate and enthusiastic action.

And in the pietist the temper of acquiescence does not always appear to the best advantage. The pessimist says in speaking of the sufferings of humanity : " Then I turned and saw all the oppressions that are done under the sun ; and behold, the tears of such as were oppressed, and they had no comforter, and on the side of their oppressors there was power, but (the oppressed) had no comforter. Wherefore I congratulated the dead more than the living that are yet alive." There is a deep pessimism there, but there is also deep compassion—there is a feeling for the wounds and sores of a bleeding humanity. But the pietist: " If thou seest the oppression of the poor and the wresting of judgment and justice in a province, do not be astonished about the matter, for every high official is guarding his own interests before another and the highest more than all." " Do not be disturbed," he says in effect, " about social wrongs and the sufferings of the poor ; they are due to the bad system of government and the corrupt self-seeking of officials." There is no pessimism there ; but there is no great compassion, no keen sympathy ; still less is there any burning indignation against an unrighteous system, or any call to arms to put down the oppressor from his seat. The pietist submits ; he is resigned ; he is calmly complacent, in face of the sufferings of the poor. And the creed which can lead to submission in such circumstances has, to say the least, something defective in it.

If the Good Samaritan, on his way down to Jericho, when he saw the man half-dead in the ditch, had not been dismayed and had said to himself, "There is nothing in this mishap to be surprised at, with all the footpads on the road and the bad policing," if he had never been moved with a compassion that drove him to an active service, he might have excelled the priest and the Levite in piety, but he would have been an object for contempt and execration, and not, as he is, for the loving admiration of mankind. There is something wanting in the piety of the pietist, and something wanting in the orthodoxy of the orthodox, who take almost as a matter of course social wrongs and the ills of men and women. For all its patient resignation and religious phraseology the creed that can permit indifference to social iniquity and social injustice, that dilutes compassion with the thought that God is over all, and does not fill the heart with surprise, and righteous indignation, and a passionate desire to right wrong, is not an ideal creed for an imperfect world, for a world in which there are the tears of the oppressed and there is no one to comfort them. A creed that allows a man to be callous or even indifferent to human wrong, that can allow the fountains of compassion to become dry and has no feeling of tenderness for the suffering and the sinful, however orthodox it may be, and whatever ecclesiastical sanction it may have, has something seriously wrong at its very heart.

The pietist, however, finds a solution for social anomalies and wrongs in a future judgment. "To everything," he says, "there is a time and judgment"; the judgment may tarry, yet it shall be well with the righteous, and punishment will certainly come to the wicked. There is to be a day of restitution when all things will be set right. But it is not much consolation to the poor and outcast, to the suffering and the

Good and Evil in the Pietist

sorrowful, to the disappointed and unsuccessful, to be told that a day is coming when they will receive compensation for all their woes. The sufferer may well ask, "When will this day be? Shall I ever see it?" And it is indeed very questionable whether a prosperity coming in some remote future can ever really compensate for the actual ills of the present. Even if the bright and happy future came, there would always be remaining the nightmare of the bitter past. An old age pension at 70 may be a cause for devout thankfulness, but it gives little relief to the poverty of the preceding five years. And what sufferers of every kind require is a present, and not a postponed, solution. The postponement may only be an additional grievance.

And, further, the solution of the pietist is somewhat crude and materialistic. The man who pleases God is not only to receive wisdom, knowledge and joy, but he is eventually to fall heir to the unjust gains of the sinner. The sinner is allowed to amass wealth, but only in the end to hand it over to the God-fearing. That no doubt would be an excellent business arrangement for the pious, and if the doctrine came to be generally accepted or could be found to have reality in fact, most people would be very pious. If the doctrine, were true, then piety would be a most excellent investment; its commercial value would be high, and there would be a big demand for shares in Piety Company, Limited. But what in such circumstances would be the moral value of the piety? Absolutely nothing. When goodness is pursued because it pays, then it virtually ceases to be goodness at all. If this doctrine, that the righteous, soon or late, prospers and the sinner has an inevitable bankruptcy to look forward to, is true, then there is really no moral world at all, for paid morality is no true morality, and bribed goodness is no foundation for a moral world.

The truth is, the pietist is a traditionalist in his religion. He has taken his creed over without question from the past and has never allowed it to be modified by the facts of life. His doctrine of prosperity to the good and ill to the wicked is the doctrine of Job's comforters, the conventional doctrine which Job himself denies. And it were futile to criticise his creed, and both futile and presumptuous to criticise the pietist himself. Whoever he was, he has gone to his reward and no longer needs, let us believe, illumination from us. It was something that in an age of hopeless depression he retained a belief in God, a spirit of reverence, an honesty in his beliefs and practices. He was not a creative genius in religion, nor a prophet fired with inspiration, nor a mystic with spiritual insight. He stuck to the old paths because no new ones were open to him. Pessimism and epicureanism were to him irreligious; wisdom, with its attempt to interpret the meaning of existence—existence that really was beyond interpretation, was simply presumptuous (vii. 24). What else could he do but hold by the old traditions? It is not easy to make new traditions, and even, if they are made, they are sometimes not as good as the old. After all, by sticking to traditions he did, as already has been said, one good thing—he helped to keep alive the Book of Ecclesiastes, and he who holds by the tradition of the past when no better offers itself is keeping alive the kernel of truth in the old tradition till such time as it shall shed its old husk and begin to germinate again in newness of life.

THE GIFT OF LIFE

Yet this (power to enjoy), according to my experience, comes from the hand of God, for who can eat or even taste anything apart from Him ?—CHAP. II. 24b, 25.

A man eats and drinks and is prosperous in his labour—but that in every case is a gift from God.—CHAP. III. 13.

No creed, which has had any sincerity in its making, is totally false. At some point or other it will find truth and help to interpret something of life's experience. The pietist was sincere in his Calvinism, and we find him touching truth when he says that whenever a man eats or drinks it is a gift of God. In saying that he has not deserted his Calvinism, which, like all Calvinism, contains some though not the whole truth. Eating and drinking is a gift—" for who can eat or drink apart from God ? "—is a true statement, almost obviously true, no matter whether it be Calvinist or Arminian, Necessarian or Libertarian, who says it, and it would still be true even though they all, with one consent, denied it.

All the machinery, if one may use the word, of mastication and digestion is presented to us, and that not in the raw material, or in different parts, but as a completely finished article. And the food and the drink, the fuel which the machinery con-

Pessimism and Love

sumes and turns into various forms of energy, are also free gifts. We are apt to think that we purchase our food by our labour, but the power to work is a gift as truly as the machinery of digestion. We buy our food and sometimes may pay for it in actual cash, but the money, artificially differentiated into earned and unearned by the tax collector, is all put into our hands. Buying and selling, exporting and importing, which is selling and buying on a national scale, is just the interchange of goods, all of which have been freely given. Whatever be the things exchanged, money on the one side or goods on the other, or goods from both changers, everything is of the nature of a presentation.

A child sometimes has a small store of money, which he calls specially his own, and out of his own money he may purchase for himself some toy, in which he is apt to think that he has distinct and peculiar rights of possession: he has bought it himself; but really it is just as much a gift, as those know who originally gave him the money, as any other toy which may have been put straight into his hands, and with the purchase of which he has had no concern. It is somewhat that way with us all. We think we have absolute rights of possession to the things for which we have paid, forgetting that the power of purchase, the article of exchange, usually money, has been put into our hands and is really a gift.

Whenever one enjoys prosperity in his labour, succeeds in his business, it is a gift of God; and yet, we speak of "self-made men!" By the expression, I suppose, we mean men who started the business of life with little or no capital standing to their personal credit, who have received little or no direct help from

The Gift of Life

others, and who, by industry and perseverance, by the exercise of energy and wisdom in their labour, have gained wealth. They have gathered their fortunes; they have made themselves what they are; they are "self-made men." But that description is very superficial, so superficial as almost to be false; it tells a mere fraction of the truth about them and their successful careers; it is a description that leaves out the most essential and important facts. For one thing, there was wealth in existence before ever this "self-made man" appeared on the scene and began to put forth his hand to grasp it; and, for another thing, before he could indulge in his prehensile activity, a hand more or less capable of prehension had to be given to him. In a word, wealth and the power to make it are gifts presupposed and indispensable for any "self-made man," and, in these circumstances, the designation is unwarranted and gratuitous. He has been presented with his living; if he succeeds beyond his fellows, he has *received* preferment from an invisible patron. Whether a man prospers little or much, it is a gift of God. No man eateth or drinketh apart from Him—an obvious truth, which, presumably, we confess in grace before meat.

The truth can be given an application beyond the range of natural and material wealth and its enjoyment. No man drinketh at the fountain of truth apart from God. There is a man of extraordinary ability and knowledge. But his learning and the mental energy with which it is acquired are things given. He does not create the truth nor the power by which he apprehends it. He is the product of truth and a capacity to receive it, and both factors are given. All our present-

Pessimism and Love

day science, of which we can be justly proud, is ours because it happens that an intelligible world—not a small thing when you come to think of it—and a corresponding intelligence, of which we are sometimes unjustly conceited, have been presented to us.

We recognise the fact that intelligence is a gift, when we call people of more than ordinary understanding "gifted." A great painter, for instance, is just a striking combination of gifts. He has sense of colour, a feeling for the beautiful, a kind of spontaneous energy of self-expression, and all are gifts. He is "gifted," but the phrase is one that can be with truth applied to every intelligent and understanding son of man. For all intellectual power, apprehension, intuition, understanding, along with the truth and facts of reality in which they work, are presented to us. No man knoweth that twice two are four, apart from God.

We sometimes say that talent is a gift, but character is acquired. A man is presented with his talents, but his character he makes himself. And so, while a man has no right to boast of his talent, he can be truly and rightly proud of his moral character. Let us, however, think of a man growing in goodness and making a character. He has a desire for goodness, and he realises the desire in a certain number of good acts, which form a good habit; in this way he may form a number of good habits, whose combined result is a good character, a character that acts on most occasions justly, purely and truthfully, and that without great strain or effort. But whether you regard the good desires or the good character in which they issue, the whole process, from its original impulse to its more or less perfect result, shows itself to be of the nature of a

The Gift of Life

gift. The good desires which are the seed out of which the fruit of character grows are a gift. They are presented perhaps along the line of heredity or of social environment, but however they came, the fact remains, they are presented. The man did not create them himself; they came to him, seed out of which a harvest of goodness could come. Or if you regard the mature product, the formed character of truth and goodness—that could never have been without the original gift of good impulse, nor without the further gift of a moral world, in which justice could be done, purity loved, and truthfulness followed.

Does this do away with moral freedom? The answer is distinctly "No," for if freedom were not given, a free gift to man, he could never have any personal moral character at all. Freedom is the power given to refuse or to receive the gift of goodness. A man can reject the gift of goodness, he can also receive it, which is the true exercise of the noble dower of freedom. Freedom, a desire for goodness, a power to attain to it, a moral world where goodness is possible, are all indispensable to character, and all are gifts. "The way of man is not in himself, nor is it in man that walketh to direct his steps," for no man doeth good apart from God.

But there is not only moral life, there is spiritual; there is not only character, there is soul. Soul expresses itself in character; but it is greater than character, it is character raised to its spiritual heights. Character may live and move and have its being within the personal and social relations of life; soul expresses itself in the same spheres, but it also rises to the Eternal realities. Soul is character in Christ and belongs to

Pessimism and Love

that new order of life which appeared in the world with Jesus. And if we go to the New Testament, which can be regarded as the first literature of the soul, we find that soul is always viewed as a gift. The Christ-informed and Christ-filled soul is a new creation, born not of flesh and blood, nor of the will of man, but of God. The eternal and Divine life of the soul is in the New Testament always a gift. Flesh and blood do not reveal or create it, but the Father in Heaven. We do not make ourselves Christian; God makes us. We do not give ourselves souls; they are the free gifts of Heaven. The Father giveth the true bread from heaven, and no man eateth thereof apart from Him.

But this is Calvinism! If it is, it is the truth in Calvinism and the truth in the creed of the old pietist of the Book of Ecclesiastes. Calvinism or no—it is the truth of experience.

Life, from centre to circumference, is a gift. And to take life in its reality as a gift leads to certain moral results of high importance. If life is a gift and really taken as such, then there will be a permanent spirit of gratitude in the heart; there will be in all the music of existence, sad or joyous, an ever-recurring refrain of thanksgiving. But gratitude, a constant spirit of thankfulness, carries so much with it in the way of moral wealth and power. Gratitude is the absolutely necessary condition of real wealth—that is, of true weal or well-being. When a man is really grateful he has what he desires, and to have what one desires is true wealth. A man is never rich, no matter how vast his material possessions may be, so long as he is ungrateful, but once he becomes grateful he is rich, abounds in true weal.

The Gift of Life

Gratitude means wealth; it also means courage; it inspires a true valour. There you are—difficulties may be crowding in upon you, or temptations may be pressing you sore, or sorrow and loss may be bruising your heart; but you are grateful, grateful that things are as they are, grateful, at least, that they are no worse, grateful that there is a hard conflict in which you can show strength, and at once the heart, though it be trembling, becomes brave to do and to dare. To take life as a gift and to take it with courage is no bad motto; and to take it as a gift means to take it with courage. The grateful are the brave.

And the grateful are the generous. Freely have they received and freely do they give. To give our life as a service we must first receive it as a gift. People who have no gratitude but that spurious gratitude which is the expectation of favours yet to come, who have no thankfulness for the past and present, but only a keen and selfish expectation of further benefits, are not among those who willingly and generously give themselves in service to their fellow-men. It is those who know that they have received life as a gift, received it freely without money and without price, that give away their own life freely, not demanding that they shall be paid for every ounce they serve.

And to take life gratefully as a gift means faith; it means the discovery of a living, loving, and personal God. Gratitude is one avenue to God. A man may be a scientific materialist, believing that the world is just one vast conglomeration of molecules, or he may be a sort of monist, holding that reality is some impersonal force or idea, that moves in endless cycles,

Pessimism and Love

but if he is grateful and takes life as a gift, he can scarcely long remain, with his heart at least, in that form of belief. Gratitude is not a feeling that can be given to matter or to any impersonal idea or force, or to ever-repeating cycles. It is a personal feeling and can only find its object in a person. Through gratitude to a loving omnipresent personal God is the line of many a man's religious experience.

Wealth, courage, generosity, and faith in a personal God are the moral implicates of true gratitude. They are the fruits of a well-planted belief that life is a gift. From the simple, obvious commonplace that whether a man eats or drinks it is the gift of God we rise to gratitude, to courage, to generosity, and to faith.

How can we realise more than we do that life is a gift ? It is obvious, but we often fail to realise the obvious. We can and we do easily deceive ourselves that our eating and drinking and all the natural joy of life are due to ourselves. We easily fancy that we pay the full price of it all. We can and we do delude ourselves about our intellectual life and its wealth and think we owe it all to our own cleverness and the marvellous energy of our own brains. But we can scarcely deceive ourselves about the soul, the Divine life in Christ, the new creation—that is, at least, beyond us, infinitely beyond flesh and blood, and is a wonder and a miracle of God alone. We cannot deceive ourselves about the soul. It is a gift, all gift, a miraculous gift. And when we have that one unmistakable gift, the pearl far beyond our price, we shall begin to realise that not only soul, but character, not only character, but intellect, not only intellect, but eating and drinking,

The Gift of Life

is a gift of Heaven. When life in its real centre is a gift the central light will diffuse itself in rays to the outer rings, and the whole will be seen to be illumined by the light and life of God. It will be all one gift; and we shall be grateful, rich, brave, generous, and among those who believe in the Eternal Love.

IV. THE SOPHIST OR WISE MAN

IV. THE SOPHIST OR WISE MAN

SOME time in the later history there arose in Israel a distinct type of character called "the wise man," a type that became a guild or a school also with the name of "the wise men" (Jer. xviii. 15). These wise men in Israel had one or two broad characteristics which marked them off both from priests and prophets. With the ritual of religion they had no concern ; nor had they any interest in the distinctly national ideals of the prophets. They were cosmopolitan. They assumed broadly the prophetic teaching as to God and duty. They looked at life and interpreted life from the human point of view, and have been aptly called "the humanists of Israel." As their name suggests, wisdom was their theme, their subject, and their muse. And they conceived wisdom in the broadest way. She was to the wise men no particular kind of skill, draughtsmanship, or ingenuity, nor was she "the slow, prudent thrift of life," but she is the whole art and science of life itself, the whole spirit that guides life to its best, richest, and happiest issues. "Wisdom is the principal thing." Wisdom is Life (Prov. viii. 35). As wisdom is the very condition of all peace, happiness, and success in life, we need not be surprised that the wise men urge that with all our getting we get wisdom.

Their urgency was doubtless a necessity. There were foolish youth and stupid age in Israel, men and women who had not learnt, perhaps would not learn, the art of true living. To such the wise men urged the claims of wisdom; to such they made her beautiful and attractive so that she might be desired. The wise men had their audience. But though the world is more than two thousand years older and has grown in experience, there appears still the same necessity to say within our own hearts and to cry upon the streets, " Wisdom is the principal thing, therefore with all thy getting, get wisdom." O man! become wise: learn the art of life.

We see men with all the means of happiness, yet without its real power; others with every opportunity of usefulness, but their usefulness is marred by some slight defect in tact or temper, which they have neither eyes to see nor wisdom to remove. We see youth losing its opportunity, blundering over its decisions in sheer stupidity of heart. We see men (and women too) taking offence over an imaginary slight, and letting it breed bitterness and misery in their hearts, taking foolish heed to what should be wisely left alone; or others uttering hard, cruel, irresponsible speech, apparently ignorant that the rebound upon themselves will be far more injurious than the blow itself. Stupidities, vanities, follies still exist—a great multitude. It is blindness, not charity, that does not see them. The cry is still necessary, " Get wisdom!"

We can see the necessity, too, when we remember how manifold, how complex is the whole duty of life. Mr. A. C. Benson, in one of his essays, says that " nothing taxes a man so heavily as the task of maintaining smooth, pleasant, and charitable relations with one's fellows." It is a tax which has to

The Sophist or Wise Man

be paid by us all, and needs wisdom for its proper discharge. Epictetus said that there is for every man one great classification of the universe, into the things which concern him and the things which do not concern him. And no doubt success in life depends on differentiating the things which concern us from those which do not—on being concerned only with our own concerns. But such differentiation makes a great and continual demand upon wisdom ; without wisdom it is impossible.

And, to take another of the common difficulties of life, how many find to make a proper and proportionate disposition of the twelve hours of the day no easy task ? They have abundance of working power and abundance of opportunity, but just through the lack of a proper and proportionate disposition of their time, they find themselves doing far too much of one thing and neglecting another altogether, to the manifest hurt of the symmetry and easy working of life. There are but twelve hours in the day, but to place them well is a tax upon wisdom. Truly life needs wisdom, therefore with all thy getting, get wisdom.

But what is this wisdom, this principal thing that is the science and art of life ? The fear of the Lord, says the wise man, is the beginning, the chief thing, the true substance of wisdom. But that answer only starts another question, What is the fear of the Lord ? The fear of the Lord, says the wise man, is to hate evil (Prov. viii. 13) ; its opposite is wisdom in one's own eyes (Prov. iii. 7), that is, it is the moral opposite of a proud, confident, intellectual superiority, it is a true humility and a willingness to learn ; further, according

Pessimism and Love

to a psalmist (Ps. v. 7), the fear of the Lord is the true spirit of worship. Blend these three, a hate of evil (which of course carries its positive—a love of the good), a true humility, and a worshipful reverence, and you have the fear of the Lord, the principal thing in wisdom. So the wise man comes simply to be the man of goodness, humility, and reverence—the man of character and religion. The question then naturally arises whether this man is wise in an actual, practical, and, using the word in the best sense, utilitarian way, whether he is a good artist working in the stuff of life, whether he is one who, in the utilitarian phrase, will make the best or most of life.

The wise men answered this question in the affirmative. Wisdom meant to them happiness, length of days, prosperity, completeness of life (Prov. viii. 35 *et passim*). And no doubt their answer was based upon experience and a careful induction. But without attempting to defend or criticise or even blame their answer, we can see thus far, that most of our mistakes in life, the mistakes that wrong our own soul, would never occur but for lack of a little of Israel's wisdom. For instance, take the mistake of being concerned with the things that do not concern us—is it not, with every one of its disastrous consequences, just due to our being wise in our own eyes, to our thinking we know everything and can do everything? The Rev. Edward Casaubon, of Middlemarch fame, was greatly concerned with details of mythology of little concern to him or anyone else, but the seed of his great useless concern was just a great conceit. He was wise in his own eyes and a fool. Or, if we look at the question not from the point of

The Sophist or Wise Man

view of mistake, but of success, we find that the people who are wise enough to gather peace and general satisfaction out of life are not for the most part of great intellect, or striking capacity, or outstanding force, but are of humble heart, grateful spirit, and reverent will. The real expert in life, the true artist in living, the genuinely wise, is the man of virtue and fear of the Lord. The whole appearance of the world and its civilisation has changed from what it was two thousand or more years ago, but wisdom is now just what it was then. Men may progress, but man and his wisdom remain the same.

But how is the true wisdom of life to come to us? Experience seems to be the natural avenue, but, as Coleridge says, " Experience is too often like the stern lights of a ship, it illuminates only the path over which we have travelled, and it gives no enlightenment or guidance for conduct in the future." We say, " Experience teaches fools " ; but it teaches them too late, when the teaching is of no value. It is not at the end of life, nor even in the middle, when wisdom is the most desirable thing, but in youth (see Proverbs *passim*). And wisdom is there at the beginning, present and accessible to youth. " Those that seek her early shall find her." She is not only present and accessible—she is urgent with her claims. She cries out on the street, asking acceptance. The wisdom of God stands at the door and knocks. The Spirit of God seeks an entrance. " If any of you lack wisdom, let him ask," and go on asking, for the hour to receive her is never too late, and never too early. Wisdom is eternally present. She comes down from above, and is more keen to enter the heart than the heart is to receive her. The wisdom of

Pessimism and Love

God, which is the wisdom of man, besets our very life.

The sophist in Ecclesiastes defends the claims of wisdom, and its worth for human life. Though most of the proverbial sayings in the book are grouped under " The Words of the Sophist," he must not be regarded as their author. He was an advocate of wisdom and a collector of proverbial sayings—the words of the wise. The pessimist also used proverbial sayings when it suited him, *e.g.*, " The crooked cannot be made straight ; and that which is wanting cannot be numbered (or made good)." The hedonist did the same, *e.g.*, " A living dog is better than a dead lion." It is for convenience' sake that not only the words spoken in defence of wisdom, but also most of the proverbial sayings are grouped under the title " The Words of the Sophist."

THE WORDS OF THE SOPHIST

And I saw that wisdom excelleth folly, even as the light excelleth the darkness.

As for the wise man, his eyes are in his head, but the dullard walketh in darkness.
Chap. II. 13, 14a.

The fool foldeth his hands together and eateth his own flesh.—Chap. VII. 5.

Better are two than one, for they have a good reward for their labour. For, if either of them falls, one can lift up his companion. Woe to the one who falls when there is not a second to lift him up! Further, if two lie together they have warmth; but how can one be warm alone? And though one alone may be overpowered, yet two will stand together and the threefold cord will not be quickly broken.
Chap. IV. 9—12.

For a dream cometh with a multitude of business and the voice of the fool with a multitude of words.—Chap. V. 3.

For dreams come through a crowd of useless activities and much talking.[1]—Chap. V. 7a.

---

[1] The text is difficult as it stands. The translation is obtained by a transposition of words.

Pessimism and Love

An advantage for the land at all times is this, a king over the worked field.[1]—CHAP. V. 9.

Sweet is the sleep of the labourer, whether he eat little or much, but the over-eating of the rich will not let him rest in sleep.—CHAP. V. 12.

A good name is better than fine nard.[2]

CHAP. VII. 1a.

Better to hear the rebuke of a wise man than for a man to listen to a song from a fool.

For as the crackling of thorns beneath the pot, so is the cackling of the fool.[2]

For extortion maketh a wise man foolish, and bribery destroys character.

Better is the end of a thing than the beginning thereof.

Better is it to be long-suffering than high and mighty.

Do not be hasty to be vexed in thy spirit, for it is in the bosom of fools that vexation finds its lodging.

Do not say " How is it that the former days were better than these ? " for it is not of wisdom that thou puttest this question.

Wisdom is a blessing with an inheritance, and an advantage to those that see the sun.

[1] Text and meaning very doubtful.
[2] In the Hebrew, there is a play on the words "name" and "nard"; also in Chap. VII. 6 on the words translated "thorns" and "pot"; another attempt to retain the play by a jingle might be "as the sound of nettles beneath the kettle."

The Words of the Sophist

Wisdom is a defence just as money is a defence, and the excellency of knowledge lies in this, that wisdom giveth life to those that possess her.
CHAP. VII. 5—11.

Wisdom is a strength to the wise, greater than the rulers in the city.—CHAP. VII. 19.

Yea, to all words that are spoken give not thy attention, for so shalt thou escape hearing thy servant cursing thee, for yea, many times thine own heart knoweth that thou thyself hast also cursed others.—CHAP. VII. 21, 22.

Who is like the wise man, and who understands the meaning of a thing? The wisdom of a man giveth light to his countenance, and the hardness of his countenance is changed.
CHAP. VIII. 1.

Yea, this have I seen as wisdom beneath the sun, and great did it appear unto me. There was a small city and few men in it, and there came a great king unto it and surrounded it and built against it great bulwarks. And there was found therein a poor wise man and he saved the city by his wisdom, but no man remembered that same poor man. Then I said, Wisdom is better than might; and the wisdom of the poor man is despised and his words are not heard.

The words of the wise heard in silence are better than the shrieking of a master among fools.

Pessimism and Love

Wisdom is better than weapons of war, and one sinner destroyeth much good.
CHAP. IX. 13—18.

One single deadly fly makes a stinking ferment in the ointment of the perfumer, and the preciousness of wisdom is destroyed by a very little folly.[1]

The understanding of a wise man is at his right hand, while the understanding of a fool is at his left.

Yea, also, whenever the fool walketh in the street his understanding fails, and he declares to every one that he is a fool.

If the spirit of the ruler rise up against thee, leave not thy place, for composure of mind allayeth great offences. — CHAP. X. 1—4.

He that diggeth a pit shall fall into it; and whoso breaketh through a fence, a serpent shall bite him.

Whoso quarrieth stones shall be hurt by them, and whoso cleaveth logs of wood shall be injured by them.

If the iron be blunt and one does not sharpen the edge, then he must put forth more strength; an advantage for success is wisdom.[2]

---

[1] The Hebrew text here needs some emendation. The translation probably brings out the sense.

[2] *Or* it is an advantage to make wise preparation.

The Words of the Sophist

If the snake bite before it is charmed, then is there no advantage to the charmer.

The words of a wise man's mouth are gracious, but the lips of a fool will bring him to confusion. From the beginning the words of his mouth are folly, and to the end an evil madness. The fool also multiplieth words: yet man knoweth not what shall be, and what shall be after him; who can tell it to him?

The attention of fools is a nuisance to him who does not know his way to the city.

Woe to thee, O land, whose king is a youth and thy princes feast in the morning.

Happy art thou, O land, whose king is the son of nobles and whose princes feast at the fitting time, as strong men without drunkenness.

Through slothful hands the beam-work sinks, and through idleness of the hands the house leaks.—CHAP. X. 8—18.

Yea, in thy thought curse not the king, and in thy bed-chamber curse not the rich; for a bird of the air shall carry the sound of thy words, and that which hath wings shall tell the business.—CHAP. X. 20.

Send forth thy bread upon the face of the waters; for thou shalt find it after many days.

Give a portion to seven, yea even unto eight;

Pessimism and Love

for thou knowest not what evil shall be upon the earth.[1]

If the clouds be full of rain they empty themselves upon the earth, and if a tree falls to the south or to the north, there, where the tree falls, let it remain.

He who is always observing the wind will not sow, and he who is always looking at the clouds will not reap.—CHAP. XI. 1—4.

In the morning sow thy seed, and in the evening withhold not thy hand: for thou knowest not which shall prosper, or whether they both shall be alike good.—CHAP. XI. 6.

Words of wise men are goads, and like nails driven in are those which form collections of proverbs.

Beware, my son; of making many books there is no end, and much study is a weariness to the flesh.—CHAP. XII. 11, 12.

---

[1] The counsel in Chap. XI. 1, 2 is to act boldly like the merchants who send forth their corn in ships, speculating on the grand scale; but, as fortune is precarious and "ships but boards" and "sailors but men," divide your merchandise. Speculate freely, but do not put all your eggs into one basket. Wisdom is distinctly practical.

TWO ARE BETTER THAN ONE

Better are two than one, for they have a good reward for their labour. For if either of them falls, one can lift up his companion. Woe to the one who falls when there is not a second to lift him up! Further, if two lie together they have warmth; but how can one be warm alone? And though one alone may be overpowered, yet two will stand together and the threefold cord will not be quickly broken.

CHAP. IV. 9—12.

This is a piece of homely wisdom, without deep pessimism or lofty idealism, the conclusion of every-day observation on a few common things in life. The words state a general truth, " two are better than one," and then continue to furnish a few illustrations chosen from the common experiences of life.

The first illustration which the sophist or wise man gives of the advantage of a second is taken from the sphere of business or industrial activity. There two are better than one, for by their joint efforts they get a good reward for their labour. By mutual suggestion, by common encouragement, by the sharing of responsibility, by the simple addition of two heads and two pairs of hands, they get better results out of their labour; they have a more prosperous business than

Pessimism and Love

if they stood alone. Says Francis Bacon: "As for business, a man may think if he will that two eyes see no more than one; or that a gamester always seeth more than a looker on; or that a man in anger is as wise as he that hath said over the four and twenty letters; or that a musket may be shot off as well upon the arm as upon a rest; and such other fond and high imaginations, to think himself all in all. But when all is done, the help of good counsel is that which setteth business straight."

The second illustration is of two travellers going along some desert path or unfrequented road: one stumbles and falls, perhaps sprains a limb; the other, a friend in need and indeed, helps him to his feet again, and, by his action, proves that "two are better than one." Or the same two travellers might get through the day without mishap: but evening comes on, and they bivouac, sleep beneath the covering of the starry heavens; they can get near to each other, and in the cold night keep one another warm. Or it might be some brigand or robber of the road appears: one man alone might have little chance of escape or defence; two might give the intruder food for reflection. Such are the sophist's illustrations of the truth that two are better than one—illustrations picked off the common road of life, where they lie thick for any man to take. A man, bathing in deep water, may take cramp; a companion near at hand would be, to say the least, a convenience. Or a man has some project to propose to his colleagues; an enthusiastic seconder is a great help towards its acceptance. Or a man is pulling a heavy load up-hill; a second to push behind will not increase the strain.

Two are Better than One

But though the sophist does not depart in his illustrations from the paths of homely and common experience, this word of his covers and has meaning for far more of life than is contained in trade or commerce, the exigencies of travel, and any obvious or ordinary situation; it is pertinent to the deeper as well as to the more superficial experiences of life—to practice and success in arts and crafts, to our personal affections, to our ideas and thinking, to morality, and to religion. In all these departments two are better than one.

Of the advantage of a second, or friend, Bacon has said again that " a principal fruit of friendship (or a friend) is the ease and discharge of the fulness and swellings of the heart, which passions of all kinds do cause and induce. We know diseases of stoppings and suffocations are the most dangerous to the body; and it is not much otherwise in the mind. You may take sarga to open the liver, steel to open the spleen, flour of sulphur for the lungs, castoreum for the brain, but no receipt openeth the heart but a true friend, to whom you may impart griefs, joys, fears, hopes, suspicions, counsels and whatsoever lieth upon the heart to oppress it in a kind of civil shrift or confession." When the heart is full of hot questionings, burdened with the weight of its own feeling, worrying, often about little or nothing, a second acts like a safety-valve and prevents that closedness which is called an eating of one's own heart, and which turns a man into a cannibal devouring his own emotions. How few people have not had some agitating experience when the feeling was, " Oh that I could tell somebody and in the telling find shrift and relief ! " In such circumstance a second would be balm, healing, and peace. And a second is of advan-

Pessimism and Love

tage to the heart, not only when it is perturbed and anxious and beset with burning thoughts, but also when it is serene and joyous and even proudly exulting for, as Francis Bacon again says, a friend " works two contrary effects ; for he redoubleth joys and cutteth griefs in halfs." If one experiences some great happiness, some joyful success, something that gives a new and brighter outlook to life, and nobody is aware of it, no one has the slightest suspicion of it, and there were no means or avenue by which a second might ever learn the fact, then the experience of happiness would be but short-lived, if indeed it were not still-born. " For they are not truly happy of whose happiness other folk are unaware." For happiness, joy, and gladness of heart " two are better than one."

And, further, for the proper and efficient working of the understanding two have great advantage over one ; for " certain it is, that whosoever hath his mind fraught with many thoughts, his wits and understanding do clarify and break up in the communicating and discoursing with another. He tosseth his thoughts more easily ; he marshalleth them more orderly ; he seeth how they look when they are turned into words ; finally, he waxeth wiser than himself ; and that more by an hour's discourse than by a day's meditation. Neither is this advantage of a second restrained only to such friends as are able to give a man good counsel : they indeed are best : but even without that a man learneth of himself, and bringeth his own thoughts to light, and whetteth his wits as against a stone, which itself cuts not. In a word, a man were better relate himself to a statue or a picture, than to suffer his thoughts to pass in smother."

Two are Better than One

But not simply for the happiness of the heart and the clarifying of the understanding are two better than one, but also for the growth and perfecting of moral manhood and womanhood. Obviously a second is of great service in the way of frank and faithful counsel on our manners, disposition, and conduct. " Dry light," said Heraclitus, " is ever the best," and there are few of us so perfect that we might not be improved by the dry light of frank criticism, free counsel, faithful reproof from a second (if we were only wise and humble enough to receive it), for however just and fair a man may try to be in the judgment of his own conduct, he can scarcely help looking at it through the moisture and mist of his own personal affection and self-prejudice. To see ourselves, our character, our disposition, our manners, in the dry light of another's judgment would be a salutary and, to most of us perhaps, a humiliating experience, though no doubt some elect and humble souls would get from the vision a moral inspiration and a blessed encouragement as from the Holy Spirit Himself.

Nor is it simply in the giving of reproof or blessed encouragement to our life of moral being and doing that two are better than one; two are absolutely necessary if there is to be any moral life at all. Moralists have sometimes divided the human virtues into self-regarding and altruistic, into virtues which we exercise chiefly or solely with reference to ourselves, and virtues which we exercise in relationship with our neighbours; but the distinction is artificial, for all virtues, even those which seem most personal and intimate to ourselves, affect our neighbours' lives, and can only be manifested or exercised in relation to them.

Pessimism and Love

In that fair cluster of the virtues—love, joy, peace, long-suffering, kindness, goodness, faithfulness, meekness, self-control—which Paul says are the fruit of the Holy Spirit there is not one that has a solely individual reference, not one that can be manifested without a second, not one that can fruit save in a social climate. To love we need some one to love ; to be kind an object for our kindness ; to be meek, gentle, or chivalrous we require a second to whom we can show these virtues. A man simply cannot have a character or a conscience at all unless he has a neighbour, a society in which it takes root, grows and puts forth flower and fruit. He may think he has made or nurtured his own character, but it has been largely in his brother's keeping and received as a gift from him. We sometimes feel that our neighbours ought to appreciate us and even be grateful to us for any goodness, kindness, or long-suffering we may happen to possess, when it is really we who ought to appreciate them and to be grateful to them for making such virtues and many others possible to us. Our character, the thing we consider the prize of life, and its price far above rubies, is ours simply because there is a second, a neighbour, men and women making for us an environment in which alone character is possible. A man cannot be good without a second. " Two are better than one."

And what is true of character is true of the soul and the soul's religion. In religion, for any religious life at all, two are absolutely necessary. To be a Christian there must be two. For what is a Christian ? A Christian in the New Testament sense is the bond-servant of Jesus Christ. His life, his talents, his character, his time and opportunities, his whole being,

Two are Better than One

are put at the service of Another, the Great Second, the Brother and Lord of every man. Without Christ a Christian is an impossibility. A Christian is not one who does this and refrains from doing that, not a man with a moral code or a string of commandments which he has piously collected and made obligatory upon himself, nor one who has prescribed a certain ritual or accepted a number of doctrines for his soul's salvation, nor even one who has attained to a certain standard of goodness or moral character, but one who, in all things, is under personal authority, a subject of an Absolute Monarch, even of Him who died for us all. As little as a man can be a loyal subject without a king, as little as one can be a servant without a master, or a youth a son without a father, so little can one be a Christian without Christ, the great authoritative Royal Second And more than this Great Second is needed ; a third is necessary, for how can one be loyal or the servant of Christ except in the service of his fellows ? The Apostle John puts the question, How can a man love God whom he hath not seen unless he love his brother whom he hath seen ?—meaning, I suppose, that the only real practical way open to a man to love God is the loving service of his brother man. And how, in what other way, can one be loyal to Christ except in the service of his fellows ? Christ, a man and his neighbour—these three are needful to the Christian life. Christ, a man and his neighbour make the threefold cord that shall not be quickly broken.

To return to the homeliness of this word of wisdom. It is a general statement and, like all general statements, has exceptions. " Two are better than one " ; that depends on who and what the second is. If the second

Pessimism and Love

of those two men travelling on a dark and lonely road happens to be a highwayman on murder intent, the first might have been safer if he had risked a solitary walk. Or if the second to whom one tells the secret burden of the heart be an incarnate news agency and universal advertiser, it had been better to have kept one's thoughts in smother. Or if the second with whom one would share one's moral and religious life be a defiant sinner and likely by his powerful wickedness to drive all virtue and grace away, in such case it were better to find another second, and in default of that to intern one's soul in Christ. Only if the second draws the best out of us, calls forth our sympathy, chivalry, truthfulness, and sacrifice, are two better than one.

And then the motive that leads one to seek a second is of importance. Why do I want a friend? Because he can serve me and my interests? Then I shall probably continue to want a friend or quickly lose him if I have the undeserved luck of finding him. Or is the motive because I want to help him and serve his interests, because there is a simple, spontaneous, pure desire to give myself to him and be my best for his sake? Then a friend will be mine.

And there is something yet more important contained and implicitly said in that word, " A threefold cord is not quickly broken." You and a second, each for the other and both for each, a twofold cord—with no thought and no affection beyond yourselves, with no high moral authority guiding and ruling your union, nothing but a dual relation—a twofold cord woven into no other strands of affection and service, it will be quickly broken and what you call love or friendship may

Two are Better than One

be turned into hate. You will not snap the cord, nor will the second, but something stronger than you both will break it ; the laws of the moral universe will burst it asunder, for the laws of the universe—God Himself —are at war against every form of selfishness, even that dual selfishness which may be called friendship or love. It is the threefold cord that cannot be broken : you and the second bound in Christ and to Him, each with your love loyal to Him and spreading itself out into the wider Kingdom of His service ; you, the second and the Christ, that union cannot be broken. That two may be really better than one, let the Christ be united to them, ruling both in their affection for each other and guiding both to a wider service. " A threefold cord cannot be broken." There is not a little wisdom in this piece of Hebrew homespun.

LUCK, OR THE ELEMENT OF CHANCE IN LIFE

The race is not to the swift, nor the battle to the strong.—CHAP. IX. 11.

It would be a mistake to suppose that these words are universally true. Most frequently, and as a rule, the battle is to the swift and the race is to the strong. If six men start to run a race the fleetest of foot will, in all probability, win the prize. Or if two armies meet each other in battle, and one is stronger than the other in numbers, in the weapons and sinews of war, and in all soldierly strength and skill, then the stronger has an almost absolute certainty of victory. The finer athlete, the better side, the more powerful army, wins in nine cases out of ten or in ninety-nine out of a hundred.

But it is not always so. The swift runner may slip or fall; he may sprain a limb; he may be " off colour " at the hour of the race and become giddy and faint; any one of a number of quite unexpected things may happen and cause him to lose the prize. In such case the race would not be to the swift. And in warfare something unforeseen, some contingency that could not possibly be counted upon, may occur, and so upset the chances of the battle that the strong goes down before the weak. In that case the battle would not be to the strong.

The Element of Chance in Life

But this proverb, this word of Hebrew wisdom, has no exclusive reference to athletics and warfare. It refers, as the words—" neither yet bread to the wise, nor yet riches to men of understanding, nor yet favour to men of skill "—which immediately follow show, to the whole race and battle of life, and in that battle and race it is no more universally true than on the field of sport and war. In life the race is most usually to the swift and the battle to the strong ; in life it is the swift of mind and the strong of body that receive the prizes. But not always so ; sometimes the swift fails in that race and in that battle the strong goes under. Robert Louis Stevenson in his " Memories and Portraits " tells the story of one of his college companions : " He was most beautiful in person, most serene and genial by disposition ; full of racy words and quaint thoughts. Laughter attended on his coming. He had the air of a great gentleman, jovial and royal with his equals, and to the poorest student gentle and attentive. Power seemed to reside in him exhaustless ; we saw him stoop to play with us, but held him marked for higher destinies ; . . . a noble figure of a youth," swift and strong, clearly destined to greatness in the race and battle of life. But, as Stevenson tells us, " somewhere on the high seas of life, with his health, his hopes, his patrimony and his self-respect miserably went down. From this disaster, like a spent swimmer he came miserably ashore, bankrupt of money and consideration ; creeping to the family he had deserted ; with broken wing nevermore to rise." Swift—the race was not his ; strong—he did not win the battle. Something unexpected, some unlooked-for chance, happened ; evidently his health

Pessimism and Love

broke, and in the breaking brought every kind of disaster.

Some seventy or eighty years ago Tennyson and Arthur Hallam were college friends. Of the two Hallam had the richer mind and gave the brighter promise. If he had lived, it has been said that he would have been one of the keenest and most distinguished intellects of Europe. But death cut him off before the world saw his light, and Hallam remained but a memory to a small circle of his most intimate friends. He was swift and strong, but the race and the battle were not his. We need not, however, go to books or literary history for illustration of the truth that " the battle is not to the swift, nor the race to the strong." Most of us can look back and see one—probably more than one—who by nature, character, and training was well fitted to take an honourable place of influence among men, to make, as we say, his mark in the world. Power, distinction, and influence seemed his certain inheritance. Whoever else might win, his victory was sure. But some chance broke his career; it might be sickness or some unaccountable moral lapse, or some circumstance or chain of circumstances, some accident from without, which could not possibly be avoided; but, whatever it was, it made the swiftness and the strength of no avail, and destroyed all possibility of prize and victory.

Nor is this the case only in the more intellectual callings of life. It occurs in business. Two men may start business together. The one has good business qualities—thoroughness, perseverance, method, tact; his qualities are supported by good opportunities, sufficient capital, a growing demand for his commodities,

The Element of Chance in Life

trustworthy and capable servants, and he succeeds: his business prospers, his wealth increases; he becomes a prince among merchants. The other possesses just as sterling qualities, insight into present demands and a foresight that can look well into the future, along with all the resources that make success practically certain; but just as he is beginning to reap his harvest of success something happens—a new discovery scraps his plant and much that it can produce, or a prolonged strike closes his works, or a war breaks out and shuts his markets, or a partner who was universally trusted proves to be a scoundrel, some bad luck or evil chance occurs, and he who was swift and strong in the stream of commerce is swept back into a small and insignificant eddy, and has to be content with a mediocre place where he has to toil hard and long for moderate results and to fight, perhaps to the end of his days, against financial deficit. "The race is not to the swift, nor the battle to the strong."

Or there are two working men. They neither of them dream of intellectual distinction or hope to build up a fortune. All they ask is a day's work, and all they want in their work is to do it decently for a decent day's pay; all they desire in their social life is a little happiness and ease, a hearth that they love and a home that is a home. They have no exaggerated ideas about themselves nor great ambitions, they are good craftsmen, seeking a day's work and a day's pay and, in the evening, a little comfort and peace. (The very salt of the country's manhood!) And one gets what he wants—his work, his pay, his hearth and home, a little leisure and comfort. He is happy and content, and, a private in the ranks of industry though he be, the

Pessimism and Love

battle is assuredly his. But with the other how different everything may be! Bad luck seems to dog his steps, evil chance to mark him as special prey; he has an accident that may cripple him all his days, or trade becomes bad again and again; and the work he wanted to do, and the modest reward he expected, and the peace he hoped for are never his; but instead of these he has days of grinding struggle, forced idleness, anxiety and bitter disappointment. It is not character that makes the great difference in their lots; it is neither willingness nor unwillingness that decides their fortunes; it is not a question of good and bad craftsmanship; it is time and chance, luck, something out of man's reckoning and control. These play their part so much in all ranks that it can be said " The race is not to the swift, nor the battle to the strong."

Now what are we to say of this element of chance, or time, or luck that appears in human life and that has not a little to do with the lot and circumstances of men, with their victories and defeats? There is one thing which it is foolish and false to say, and that is that life is all chance and that luck decides all the fortunes and issues. That is not true. A man may have all the luck, time and chance may almost thrust the prize into his hand, and yet he may fail and may win not a laurel leaf, no power, no influence, no future, no comfort, not even respect and respectability. He has all the luck, but he lacks the character, and the luck cannot make good what the character has lost. Another may be no favourite of chance and fortune, but he has determination and strength, and wins perhaps not a first prize, nor even a second, but a decent place in the race and battle—gains enough, at least, to make the

The Element of Chance in Life

battle a joy and cause for thankfulness. Luck is not everything. Chance is not king and only lord of man's lot. It plays a part on the stage of life, but not the chief *rôle*. To say that it does is not simply to be cynical, but it is to show a lack of perception and a blindness regarding the facts of life.

And, further, the chance that withholds the race from the swift and the battle from the strong is not an altogether evil thing. It may rob a man of the prize on which his heart is set, but it may give him in its stead a far richer prize. I referred to the picture which Robert Louis Stevenson gives of his college chum, whose natural destiny was destroyed by some apparently evil chance. But it would not be fair to that friend of Stevenson's, though we only know him from a beautifully worded picture, to leave the picture where I did, for that was only half the picture. In his rich, strong, and swiftly moving life we are told that there was something soulless, a certain incredulousness of good, a slight dash of cynicism, not much of a taint, a mere spot almost invisible on so glorious a sun. But when chance ruined him, when something stronger than himself brought him low, "in his face there was a light of knowledge that was new to it. Of the wounds of his body he was never healed ; died of them gradually with clear-eyed resignation ; of his wounded pride we knew only from his silence. He returned to that city where he had lorded it in his ambitious youth ; . . . at times still grappling with that mortal frailty that had brought him down ; still joying in his friends' successes ; his laugh still ready but with kindlier music ;—to his last step, gentle, urbane and with the will to smile. The tale of this great failure is, to those

Pessimism and Love

who remained true to him, the tale of a success. In his youth he took thought of none but himself; when he came ashore again, his whole armada lost, he seemed to think of none but others. Often have we gone to him, red-hot with our own hopeful sorrows, railing on the rose leaves in our princely bed of life, and he would patiently give ear and wise counsel; and it was only upon some return of our own thoughts that we were reminded what manner of man he was to whom we disembosomed: a man . . . ruined; shut out of the garden of his gifts; his whole city of hope both ploughed and salted; silently awaiting the Deliverer. Then something took us by the throat; and, to see him there so gentle, brave and pious, oppressed but not cast down, sorrow was so swallowed up in admiration, that we could not dare to pity him." Some chance—was it a dash of cynicism or some physical weakness? We know not; but it shut him out from the prize and victory. An evil chance? No; for it gave him a new spirit, a spirit triumphant over all chance and every evil thing.

Nor was the chance that slew Arthur Hallam long ere his prime an altogether evil thing. It brought his friend face to face with the mysteries of sorrow, loss, and death. It made him ponder these great mysteries till their darkness became a light; till over the grave he saw a risen Christ bearing life and immortality in His hand, and till his despair was turned into hope and power to sing the triumph over death, and to sing it with such persuasion as to confirm many in a victorious faith and " larger hope." And so Hallam, by the chance that smote him, has done more for the world than by a life of a longer day which might

The Element of Chance in Life

have brought to him success upon success, prize upon prize. Take any life that has been let or hindered by chance, shut out by accident of fortune from prize and victory, kept humble and obscure by circumstances over which it has no control, and by its very hardship and apparent failure been taught patience and the habit of living from within, out of the wells of an inward strength and sufficiency. What does such a life do for us ? It gives us a sense of man's real greatness, of his greatness independent of every external trapping ; it gives us a feeling of inspiration that does not come from the gloriously successful and it makes those who greatly prosper and whose bed is on the roses and lilies of life humble and reverent.

Suppose that there were no such thing as chance, or time, or luck, no accident, no uncontrollable circumstances that can stop or impede a man's career and change the whole conditions of his lot. Suppose the race was always to the swift and the battle always to the strong. Would it be gain or loss ? It would undoubtedly be loss. For in such case we should all take our lives into our hands, fighting in our own strength and running in our own swiftness. We should be without an element in life that intimates to us that there is something greater than ourselves in the world, a Power that is greater than all our powers and that can defeat our strength, without something that tells us that we are but men and God is God. If the race were always to the swift and the battle always to the strong we should come to the awful idolatry of strength and swiftness, and of the prize and victory that strength and swiftness bring. What keeps us from despising the unsuccessful man ? The fact that we

Pessimism and Love

know that time and chance happen to all men and that a man may be good and true and faithful even though he has not succeeded according to the common idea of success. And what keeps us from worshipping the simply successful man ? The fact that we know that his prosperity may be due largely to time and chance, and we must look behind the prosperity to see if there is virtue and goodness before we honour him and give him virtue's praise.

Blind chance ? It is not blind ! It is we that are blind ! We see not whence chance cometh nor whither it goeth. We do not see it in perspective nor how it bears upon the whole of life. There is a town which I know well. It is no garden city. It is dark in appearance, and its buildings, huddled together, are not imposing. As one walks its streets on a day of mist and rain it creates an impression of God-forsakenness. But behind the town there is a hill, and if one will take the trouble to ascend and from the top look down it bears a new aspect. Beyond its bleak-looking and black houses and irregular streets there is a glorious wealth of sea whence the breakers come and beat almost on the very thresholds of the houses, and you see the river, that appears so dirty as you look at it from the main street, meandering in its upper reaches through meadows and linking the town to scenes of pastoral peace, while the smoke from the chimneys and the echoes of human voices add vitality to the whole scene. It is a pleasing picture. The town is only mean when you are near it and beholding it with short-sighted vision. Ascend and view it in its surroundings, it does not depress one with its gloom ; it seems a good place for one to have his home. Get up to the heights and

The Element of Chance in Life

view what we call "bad luck" in its perspective, in its effects upon the whole of life, and you will see it adds to the richness and depth and the very joy of living. You will see chance, not as blind, but as part of the open-eyed providence of God.

But there is one sphere of life where the race is to the swift and the battle is always to the strong—the sphere of character. "Blessed are those that hunger and thirst after righteousness, for they shall be filled." No chance, no accident, no external circumstance, can prevent that result. If a man lives for righteousness, righteousness will be his. In the very desire for righteousness he is righteous. To seek Christ with the whole mind and will is to find Him. In the sphere of character and in the life of the spirit " whatsoever a man soweth, that shall he assuredly reap."

THE ELEMENT OF RISK IN LIFE

He that diggeth a grave shall fall into it.

He that breaketh down a wall, a serpent shall bite him.

He that quarrieth stones shall be hurt by them.

He that splitteth logs of wood will be endangered through them.—CHAP. X. 8, 9.

The meaning of these words is, that if a man is digging, he may come by an accident, he may fall into the pit or hole at which he is working; if he is pulling down a wall, a serpent, lying as serpents like to do between the damp stones or bricks or mud, may give him a bite; if he is a quarryman quarrying stones, he is liable to be hurt at his work; if he is a woodcutter, cleaving logs of wood, he is engaged at a dangerous trade. The delver, the mason, the quarryman, the sawyer, each at their several jobs, run risks, the dangers of their occupation. Their trades are all more or less dangerous. The words state simple facts of common experience.

But manifestly they are meant to express not merely a few simple well-known facts, but also the general truth that in almost every occupation, situation, or calling there is an element of risk or danger, which, in some cases at least, is sure to become actual; that is, there is not only risk, but wounds,

The Element of Risk in Life

pain, suffering, loss connected with practically every kind of occupation or calling in life. The builder has the builder's risk—he may be erecting a house, and a beam or weighty stone may fall upon him and crush him; the quarryman has dangers in his occupation; the sawyer has his. The sailor, the miner, the engineer, the railway worker, the maker of explosives, the soldier are engaged in highly dangerous occupations, while some other workers, as we know, do not run the same risk, they are not liable to the same degree of accident. But nearly all trade, all work in mill or mine, on land or on sea, is exposed to a certain amount of danger varying with the nature and circumstances of the occupation. And even if the workman escapes accident, gets clear of the risk, there is a constant drain on his energy, a slow exhausting of his physical life, which may not be felt in the early days of exuberant youth and of strong manhood, but which begins to tell and be painful after middle life is reached, going on in its wearing process till it leaves the workman, as we say, "a done man." That is the truth which these four proverbial sayings record—a truth which covers and is applicable to more than manual labour or physical employment.

For instance, there is a business man; he may be prospering, adding to his capital and to his yearly income; his prosperity, his increased capital is, as this Book of Ecclesiastes says, "a defence"—it protects his business from financial accident; but if he is taking a broad outlook as to the purpose of his business—that it is a means not only for his own making of money, but a means of providing others with work and wages, which will secure

Pessimism and Love

for them and for their families the necessities of life, that, in a word, his business is a channel by which his workmen and the community are served—he may, with this broader outlook in mind, extend his business, launch out into new enterprises and ventures, through some of which he may suffer loss and be seriously wounded in his resources. He runs risks and he may suffer from the risks. Or, if his loss does not come in that way, he may have crises of grave anxiety, and all the time, in days of prosperity as well as in days of declining business, he has a weight of care, a burden of responsibility that is continually, to use a common phrase, "taking it out of him." An outsider may think that, with the defence which capital gives, he is immune from every care, protected from almost every danger; but if he were to tell the whole true story of his experience in business, there would be, in all probability, a revelation of a few things not easy to bear, of honourable and necessary risks run and of wounds received. Or to take an illustration of a different character—the social reformer. He would pull down walls of prejudice, injustice and hurtful things, and a serpent will bite him; he will be misunderstood, his motives will be suspected and challenged, and the very people to whom he would bring and does bring blessing may have little or no gratitude and may only think he might have done more than he has. He who would serve the community will have irritations to bear; ignorant criticism, old prejudices, will rise up against him—the serpent will bite him; he need not think that he will be immune. Every situation has its serpents that bite: it has dangers; it has injuries, irritations, strains, and stresses, that take the life (in many cases

The Element of Risk in Life

the mental and spiritual far more than the physical) out of the worker, putting heavy toll on his energy, on his patience and power to suffer.

What is one to say of these wounds and bites, these risks and dangers, that are encountered in every walk of life and which, in so many cases, bring suffering and loss? When the suffering becomes greater and more serious than usual we may ask whether the labour through which it came was worth while. A man may quarry stones till his back is bent, and, as he thinks of his crippled condition, may be forgiven if he questions the utility to himself of all his days of hard toil—quarrying stones his life long for a bent back! Or a man may come by some severe accident, be grievously wounded in an explosion or torn in the whirring machinery, and as he thinks of the days of wearisome inactivity that lie before him he may ask, Was it all worth while for such a mutilated result? And the answer, surely the answer is, No! it was not worth while. It is of little or no utility to the worker to dig a pit to fall into it, or to pull down a wall to be bitten by a serpent, or to quarry stones to be hurt by them, or to split wood and be injured at the task. It is not worth while to go to war to be wounded; it is still less worth while to go to war to be killed. And we should imagine it to be a distinctly unpleasant experience for the delver to tumble into the trench he is digging, or for the builder to find a beam or half a roof surely descending upon him, or for the quarryman to be injured in the blasting operations, or for the sawyer to be lacerated by the saw. So unpleasant in experience and so trying in the consequences that one scarcely is surprised at the question, " Was it worth while? "

Pessimism and Love

But it is questionable whether one would remove all those risks and dangers, even if one could, which are connected with the commonest duties and callings of life, and which mean, to some, loss, hurts, wounds, and even death. It is doubtful whether one would make all the work of life absolutely without danger, protected against every possible risk. Some time ago I was stranded waiting for the midnight mail at a station in the North of England. There was little movement in the station, a stray porter would appear, evidently for the purpose of banging a door, and then disappear; occasionally a shunting train or its engine's whistle made itself heard. Waiting in these somewhat gloomy and solitary circumstances I heard a train come in at a distant part of the station. I wondered what this could be, for I thought that the London mail was the only train expected at that hour of night. Very soon I learnt the meaning of the train, for no sooner had it drawn up than I heard the march of the clogs echoing through the empty and gloomy station, not one pair of clogs, but a hundred or even two hundred—an army of miners coming off their shift. I went to a point where a light was shining, and watched this army march past to the tune—the clack-clack—of the clogs. There they passed blackened and begrimed, each man with his pannikin and his lamp. I looked into their faces and marked, as well as the fleeting impression would allow, their mien and gait. The march was quick; there was no lagging; there was little or no speech among them; there was a grim, absorbed, keen look on almost every countenance. I doubt if one man noticed my presence, as I stood alone and right under the light. They came forth out of the night to the sound of the clogs

The Element of Risk in Life

and into night again they passed to their echoes. I began to ponder first as to where these men were going, to the long rows of small cottages with their dreary back yards, some of them, alas! to little comfort within the home, and then I thought of where they would go again on the morrow. Where? To the pits!—And if a man dig a pit he shall fall into it—to duty, risk and danger. And I said to myself that black horde are heroes all. "They get used to it," does someone say? That does not affect the heroism. "They think nothing about it." But that is the spirit of true valour. They know the risks; they know that if a man diggeth a pit he may fall into it. But they go—used to it and thinking nothing about it; dig the pits, descend into the deeps of the earth—surrounded every shift with dangerous probability: they go, heroes all. But were there no risks and no dangers, were it not for the fact that when a man digs a pit he may fall into it, there could be no valour, no heroism. The risks and the dangers make the miners a veritable army, the Black Watch of the deeps of the earth.

Would one remove all the risks and dangers from the ordinary callings, trades, occupations in which men engage? Would one have every field of labour bloodless and woundless? Would one do away with all possibility of personal sacrifice? No! For it is just because a man who diggeth a pit may fall into it, or one who pulls down a wall may be bitten by a serpent, just because the quarryman may lose limb or life, and the woodman may be hurt in his occupation—simply through the universal risk that there is the opportunity for the spirit of valour and heroism in the common vocations and duties of every-day life. The field of

Pessimism and Love

battle is reckoned the field of valour just because if a man fights with the foe he may be wounded, he may be slain ; but there are possible wounds, possible suffering, and possible death on every field of the world's work and struggle, and so every field is the field of valour. Valour, the spirit of the brave, of the courageous unto death, who would remove that ? The dangers, the wounds, and the losses are the price we pay for it, and the price is not too great. The social reformer has to face the risk of being charged with false motives, the bites of prejudice and the wounds that ingratitude makes ; but were it not for these he would be without opportunity for moral heroism and righteous daring: it is the risks which give him his chance of playing a hero's part. Who would remove them ?

But the dangers and risks do even more than call forth the spirit of valour. Many of them are preventable, and they have called forth man's skill and ingenuity. The perils of the sea have compelled men to plan and devise their defeat ; they have brought the lifeboat into existence and forced man to resolve to become, as far as possible, lord and master of the great waters. Many of the great scientific inventions are ours because man has had to face such dangers and risks as have compelled him to use his utmost ingenuity to defeat them.

But that is not all ; the perils and wounds of every-day life create the spirit of sympathy. We have in our country to-day a Workmen's Compensation Act, which is the expression of a nation's compassion for those who have to dig or build or hew or work in mill or mine, for those who have to labour and who may be wounded in their labour.

The Element of Risk in Life

We have, too, an Old Age Pensions Act that is the expression of a people's sympathy for those who have to toil and who grow old and weak in their toil, for those who work and who die daily at the work they do. These two Acts are like great deposits of national compassion, and the national heart is all the richer for them.

The dangers call forth valour and they call forth ingenuity and compassion, but even that is not all. The miner who works in the deeps of the earth, the sailor who does his business in great waters, the man who plies the shuttle or tends the loom, tillers of the soil, engineers, builders, sawyers, soldiers on the field of battle, are all engaged in a great service. They serve their loved ones; they provide hearth and home, food and raiment, they are the breadwinners for those who are dependent upon them. They serve their own homes; they also serve the community. Those miners, for instance, that go to the pit where they may fall keep the mills of Lancashire working; they are the mainspring of our great traffic system; their work is a condition of comfort in every home of our land. It is a great service in which they are engaged—a service that is turned into a noble sacrifice of love by the very risks and dangers of their occupation. They can be wounded in their service; they can be slain in their duty; they can and do serve unto death. It is a service with an obedience and a love unto death in it, a service that is a sacrifice for others' good. The risks and the dangers call forth valour, skill, compassion, and holy sacrifice. Who would remove them? The ordinary plains of life's duty are fields for the chivalrous, the heroic, and the sacrificial. We can praise God for the dangers that make them such.

Pessimism and Love

The wounds are there in the Christian life. If one become a Christian, a servant of the Lord Jesus Christ, he will not be shot, nor burnt, nor sawn asunder. But there is a cross, there are wounds, stings, self-effacements ; but it is just these things that make the Christian life chivalrous and courageous, that make it a life of love and sacrifice. There are trials in the Christian life, but count it all joy when ye fall into manifold trials ; these are your opportunity for valour ; nay, is there not in them a veritable incitement and an additional allurement to follow the King ?

A PLEA FOR SELF-CULTIVATION

If the iron be blunt and one do not whet the edge, then must one put forth all the more strength. It is an advantage to make wise preparation.—CHAP. X. 10.

Linguistically this verse is one of the most difficult in Ecclesiastes. The sense is, however, plain, and I would translate, " If the iron be blunt and one do not whet the edge, then must one put forth all the more strength. It is an advantage to make wise preparation."

If a woodman be felling trees, or a reaper be mowing grass, and the axe or the scythe lose its edge, it is a wise thing for the workman to sharpen his tool. To do so will save labour and energy and give more ease, dexterity, and happiness in the work. A good workman, if only for his own sake, will keep his tools in workable condition. It can only be sheer, stupid, slothful obstinacy that will let a man go on with his scythe all the day and never apply the whetstone. The grass will not be so clean cut, his back will ache more from the extra labour, and, by evening, the scythe will have lost its edge altogether and be practically useless until it has received more than ordinary attention. And then it is foolish to go on swishing with the scythe and never break the monotony or get a restful change by periodic whetting. Whetting acts like a series of

Pessimism and Love

small inspirations to the worker in his toil; it gives him fresh starts with a keen blade fit for its work. And what is true of scything or felling trees is true of most crafts and trades. Tools in good working order, well-kept machinery, are an advantage to the workman, an advantage which a good workman will take care to have. And tools reveal the workman. If the tools are rusty or blunt you can have little faith in the user. But if they are kept in good working order, sharp and clean, they declare a wise man who has pride in his work. A fool is careless and slipshod; but a wise workman looks to the perfection of his tools, for the sake of his own ease, happiness, and skill as well as for the sake of the perfection of the work itself.

But this word is a proverb, and while it tells the reaper to be wise and keep his scythe keen, and the woodman to sharpen his axe and every craftsman to look to his tools, it suggests a wider range of thought and activity. It inculcates the wisdom of preparing and making fit all the tools, the instruments and the powers, that men use in the whole business of life. It is an advantage that tells in every sphere of duty and activity to make wise preparation, to have one's tools in good condition.

Life as a whole may be regarded as a vocation, presenting a work which is to be done. For this work certain tools or instruments have been given, which, if they become dull and one do not whet them, one has inevitably to put forth the more strength. For instance, there is the instrument of Intelligence. We believe in sharpening that tool. It is a kind of sacred, no less than legal, obligation to educate our children, to train and draw out the powers of their intelligence, so that

A Plea for Self-Cultivation

they may have tools prepared and fit for the work of life. If the obligation is not fulfilled our children will be but common hodmen in the work of life, hard slaving plodders with no sense of ease, dexterity, and joy in their activity. We can scarcely give too much thought or consideration to the training of youthful intelligence, to the whetting of its understanding. But with some people the only whetting their intelligence gets is that which has been compulsorily received in the days of their youth. The door of the school or the college has closed upon them for the last time, and they go out into the world, as we say, to their life's work. They enter their business or occupation ; they do its tasks and meet its obligations, and for these a certain amount of intelligence is necessary ; but they are quite satisfied with what they have got—it does their turn. They scarcely ever read a book that might enlarge both their knowledge and their imagination ; they never attend a lecture unless it be concerned with their own business and is likely to teach them how to make more money ; they never allow their intelligence to wander out of the beaten every-day tracks ; never give it a holiday in some land of imagination and beauty ; never let it climb a mountain to get a new and more extensive view of life : they keep it to the narrow paths of daily activity ; they swing the scythe—they never stop to whet it. The result is that they have to put forth more strength. Their work becomes a monotonous toil and a toilsome monotony. The material rewards, the pay, which they receive, or the profits which they make, do not remove the weariness.

Take a concrete instance. Here is a man who has an occupation, some trade or profession. He attends to it

Pessimism and Love

with regularity. No one could accuse him of neglect. He is not slothful. He gives the most of his day and all his energy to his work. He goes through the routine and the drudgery as though they were a second nature to him. He puts his intelligence into his work; indeed, all his intelligence is strictly confined to his daily duties. But let such a one stop. Let him put to his intelligence some such question as this: " What is the meaning of this work I am doing ? What is the purpose of my business ? " Let him cease to be active in that practical, mechanical way of his; let him become receptive. Let him think over his work or his business, not in a businesslike, commercial way, but in a larger and more imaginative spirit. Well; what is he doing ? Let him think. He is serving the community; he is supplying their comfort and meeting their needs; he is distributing the gifts of God to God's children; he is a " middleman " between God and members of the family of mankind. He is himself a servant of God. What is he doing ? Selling goods, trafficking in merchandise ? Yes; but in the process he is putting certain great moral principles into action—honesty, faithfulness, perseverance, patience; putting them into practice and making them part of his very nature and life. In his business, if he will only think and whet his wits, he will see that he is gaining character— character that is far beyond the price of rubies and worldly wealth. If he will only sharpen his imagination, he will see a new glory in his business and daily occupation. And now let him turn that whetted intelligence again to his work. Will not his work be easier ?—a more attractive, a more joyful, thing ? Will there not be a music in the very monotony of it ?

A Plea for Self-Cultivation

Will there not be a new privilege and a new gratitude ? The old weariness will depart, and he will give thanks for the work that lies to his hand and that is a joy to his heart.

There are more ways, however, of whetting the intelligence than the method of reflection. Reflection is not an easy thing for any of us, still less for those who are immersed in practical things and to whom it is not a habit. But there are " aids to reflection." Let the practical worker read what more imaginative and reflective souls have thought and said about the meaning and purpose of the work, duties, business, and occupation of life ; let him read the story of some of the finest and best workers ; let him learn the spirit and the motives in which they worked ; let him discover the large, grand, yet humble conceptions which they had of their work, and his intelligence will be sharpened, his work will become easier and be better done. The whetted scythe will have a new power and carry a new inspiration. Always to be doing, doing, doing, and never thinking, never reflecting, never using imagination—that means the iron becomes dull and he has to put forth more strength.

Another instrument that has been given us for the carrying through of the work of life is Conscience. Conscience is the faculty that tells us what is right and morally preferable and urges us to do it. It guides us through the sometimes intricate ways of moral duty, and leads us into the path which is good and where our peace and happiness lie. It brings us, or seeks to bring us, into true and satisfactory relations with one another. It is a gift given to every man. We sometimes say a man is without conscience. He can

Pessimism and Love

cheat and lie without compunction, but you try and cheat him and you will see how very conscientious he becomes, how much conscience there then is in him, how much true knowledge of right and wrong. But conscience is not a perfected faculty with any of us. It is, in all of us, capable of development, of nurture, of growth, of education, of enlightenment. There are people who act quite conscientiously and pride themselves on their conscience, and yet do wrong, and of all wrongdoing, conscientious wrongdoing is the most mischievous and obstinate. They have conscience, but it is an uneducated, undeveloped, unsharpened one. Unless conscience is continually whetted, it becomes blunt and will make mistakes for which penalty will have to be paid.

So-called conscientious people are often morally stupid, obstinate, and unjust in their judgments and in their actions. The truth is not one of us has any right to put an absolute trust in our conscience, unless he is whetting it to a finer edge, unless he is continually making it a truer and more sensitive instrument. Take a common instance. Some people pride themselves on the fact that they say what they think; their conscience bids them to be courageous in their speech, and they do say what they think, things which sometimes wound, but as their conscience has told them to say these things, they are morally satisfied with themselves. But if they had whetted their conscience, made it more sensitive, given it a little more insight and sympathy, their conscience, so far from telling them to say what they think, would authoritatively forbid them even to think what they say. Few of us are there who cannot look back to

A Plea for Self-Cultivation

some action, or course of action, of which we can say, " I could not blame my motives, but, all the same, the action was wrong and I had to pay the penalty." If our conscience had been a little more enlightened, it would have had other and different motives, and we should have acted quite otherwise.

How are we to whet our conscience ?

By getting rid once and for ever of the idea that in matters of conscience we have attained perfection and that our moral judgments are final and absolute. So long as we think we are right, always right, and that all we need to do is to appeal to our conscience, and right judgment and right action will follow ; so long as we think that, our conscience will be blunt and we shall have to put forth more strength, in this case more self-assertion, which, to say the least, will not increase the winsomeness and charm of our moral life. We must be willing to learn ; we must have the teachable heart of little children.

Codes of moral law are of little avail in teaching the conscience. Text-books on conduct are of small profit. But the influence of people who have nobler, purer, and better-informed consciences than ourselves may act like a whetstone upon our moral sense. Simply to read the story of some pure and devoted life may illumine our heart and moral judgment and give us greater moral understanding and a new inspiration. If we are only willing to learn, if we have the courage not only to hold to our moral convictions but to change them when we are wrong, we shall find in every noble act, in every bit of faithful service, in every true and noble heart, a whetstone for our conscience. Our conscience can become blunt and mechanical, it can

Pessimism and Love

work more by force than fineness of perception; but to be effective for the delicate and varied relations of life it must be constantly disciplined, educated, sharpened to finer judgment and more delicate action, and that without losing its strength.

Another gift, the highest and greatest of all given for the work of life, is the Soul. And as it is true that every man has a conscience, so it is true that every man has a soul. Soul—that is, the power to know God and to live in union and communion with Him—that is the property of every son of man. It is true that some men have got what is called a genius for religion and others a capacity poorer and more limited; but in all there is a spark of Divine life which may kindle into a great flame and blaze into a great light. The soul recognising and unfolding to spiritual realities and relations is a gift from Heaven to every son of man. But the soul may become blunt; it may lose its sensitiveness to eternal things; it may lose its hold of those great, unseen forces of Love and Holiness, of God Himself, by which man truly lives. And then man has to put forth more strength; life becomes darker and harder with more weariness and less inspiration in it. The soul lays hold for us of the powers of patience, courage, sacrifice, love and faith, and without these we are fools and blind, poor stumbling hodmen in the work of life.

> " Our sacred selves ! Have we
> No charge to keep o'er this divinity
> That lives within us ? "

A great charge. A charge to whet our souls by prayer and worship, by communion, by living contact with the souls of men and with the soul of Christ.

THE FABLE OF THE CHARMER AND THE SNAKE

If the snake bite before it is charmed, what advantage hath the charmer?—CHAP. X. 11.

These words seem very like the "skeleton of a fable," of a fable precipitated, as it were, into the form of a proverb; and to put some flesh and blood on the skeleton, to dissolve the proverb back into a fable, is not a difficult task.

There was once a snake-charmer famed for his knowledge of every creeping thing and for his power over them. In presence of his skill and wisdom the most venomous reptile became harmless as a dove. He had only to utter his spell and the most vicious cobra, hissing forth its hate and coiled in readiness for its fatal spring, fell limp to the earth; its eyes lost their gleaming hate; and it slowly crawled, as in act of meek and dutiful obedience, to its lord. Such skill brought the charmer wealth and great renown. Kings and the great in the land honoured him, and he became proud and slothful of spirit. On one occasion the charmer was in an uncommonly vain and careless mood, and, in the presence of a snake, he failed to speak the incantation, whereupon the snake sprang and bit its lord, so that he who had such power died of the wound. The people in their ignorance scoffed at the skill of the charmer, saying, "What availeth the charmer and the charmer's

Pessimism and Love

spell ? He is no better than we." And a new fear of creeping things got hold of their heart.

In the form of some such fable this proverb may possibly have once existed, setting forth the lesson that knowledge is of little use unless the wise man puts it into practice, that, by itself, it will not save from bites and wounds and destruction. To apply the fable, either in its (possibly) original and extended form or in its proverbial and aphoristic precipitate or sediment would not be difficult in the times when Ecclesiastes was written and the schools of Hebrew wisdom flourished. There were many men full of wise saws and instances, men who made it their business to collect words of wisdom which were supposed to save from all the wounds, bites, and evils of life and to lead into the way of happiness and peace. But suppose some of these men did not apply their gathered wisdom, suppose they did not put into practice the wisdom which they had learnt and which they most zealously preached to others, what then ? Their wisdom was of little or no advantage to them. The wise man in that case was no better than the fool. The wisdom which should have been a defence, a guidance, and a salvation was useless, and with its professors was in danger of falling into evil repute. Wisdom by itself availeth nothing. To be of use it must be put into practice. Such, then, is the teaching of this " skeleton of a fable," this fable in the form of a proverb, " if the serpent bite before it be charmed then is there no advantage to the charmer."

Modern application of this proverb-fable is not difficult to find. There is a man with great power to gather knowledge ; the acquisitive faculty is strong

The Charmer and the Snake

in him, and, in obedience to its impulse, he gathers facts from every field; he is acquainted with the science of to-day, has the history of the past in his memory, knows ancient civilisations and understands modern institutions. He is a man of learning, of encyclopædic knowledge, himself a veritable encyclopædia. But you feel that there is something deficient about him. You wonder at his powers of acquisition and memory, you admire them, you stand aghast at his prodigious learning, but the man himself does not seem, for all his great intellectual possession, one whit the happier or more successful in the broad art of life. Those vast stores of knowledge do not appear to bring him more light or guidance than ordinary men possess; they do not make him a better companion, or a truer friend, or even a more trustworthy guide for others in the everyday business of life. His knowledge does not seem to act as a helm nor even as ballast, but rather as a hindering and hampering dead-weight to his life. He belongs to the kind of character which has been made immortal in the portrait of the Rev. Edward Casaubon, of " Middlemarch " fame. Casaubon was a very learned man; he was engaged on a vast intellectual scheme, the collection of the mythologies of ancient peoples and their scientific arrangement for some vague purpose or other concerned with their unity of origin. He spent years over his gigantic intellectual work. He impaired his sight through it; he lost his health. But all who know Casaubon feel that he would have been a better sort of man if he had never touched mythology at all. His prodigious knowledge did not save him from small jealousy and petty spite; it did not enlarge his sympathy and the understanding of his heart; it did

Pessimism and Love

not teach him how to bear the disappointments and trials of life with courage ; it did not make him a boon companion or a choice friend, or in any way a lovable character. When you do not feel contempt for him, you only profoundly pity him. His knowledge strikes you not merely as useless, but worse than useless, a positive evil. It saved neither him nor his friends from the bites and wounds of life. And no doubt to those who have the courage to think so, the Rev. Edward Casaubon was simply an omniscient fool. He had knowledge, tons of it, but never an ounce found practical and beneficial application.

In a practical age like ours the uselessness of un-applied intellectual knowledge will be readily granted. But the sophist who has preserved for us this fable-proverb, was not thinking of intellectual knowledge, of what we call science, but of a wisdom of a more practical and moral order. He was thinking of such wisdom as is contained in the Book of Proverbs, a wisdom which is above rubies and which a wise son will hear from his father, a wisdom that inculcates a humble willingness to learn, that will hearken to instruction and bear reproof gladly, a wisdom which teaches purity, truthfulness, the fair balances of honesty, the duty and profit of industry and the fear of the Lord. Now a man might be a most apt pupil in this school of wisdom ; he might know many collections of proverbs by heart and be well versed in the sayings and instruction of those who were wise in the art of life. More than that, he might assent to the truth and profit of this moral wisdom and be loud in its praise. A brilliant pupil, he might become a leader and a master in a school of wisdom. But for all his wisdom, his knowledge of

The Charmer and the Snake

moral instruction, and his willing and whole-hearted assent to the principles of the wise men he might himself fail by falling into some of the snares and traps against which wisdom so strenuously warned him; he might, while praising the wisdom that says lying lips are an abomination to the Lord and deceitful balances His abhorrence, be what we call " a very slippery customer " whose word needed confirmation at the mouth of two witnesses at least before it could be finally accepted. He might recite with an unction well-nigh tragic those terrific warnings against sensualism and yet be guilty of great folly. Solomon himself, whose wisdom " excelled all the children of the East and all the wisdom of Egypt, for he was wiser than all men, . . . and whose fame was in all the nations, and who spoke three thousand proverbs and whose songs were a thousand, and who spake of trees from the cedar that is in Lebanon, even unto the hyssop that springeth out of the wall, and who spake also of beasts and fowl, and of creeping things and fishes and to whose wisdom all people came to hear "—Solomon himself the great botanist, the distinguished naturalist, the perfect moralist, the patron of wisdom and himself the ideal wise man—is himself hard hit by this proverb, for the very snake against which his own wisdom warns bit him with a poisonous and deadly bite.

It is possible to possess the wisdom of moral principles and ideals and to fail to put them into practice, possible to be a theoretical moralist, noble in ideals, but mean in deeds. There is an episode in one of Tourgenieff's novels where a noble lady is seated in her carriage reading a story of tragic suffering and weeping piteous tears over the woeful tale, while her coachman is slowly

Pessimism and Love

freezing to death on the box and is eventually found a corpse. It is possible to have the most sublime and heavenly sentiments, and yet not one of them ever waters the earth with a real and saving compassion : it is possible to know the ten commandments, to consider them a most wonderful and complete code of morals, and yet more than one of them may fail to have vital authority and power over the life : it is possible to have the noblest ideals, to delight in them and sing their praise, but there their practical efficiency may end.

The fool, says the sophist in another place, does not know his way to the city. In going to the town where he lives he may lose not only his path but himself. He may conduct himself like a fool, speak the wrong word and do the wrong thing, and return home with a harvest of trouble and anxiety to himself. Such is the fool, and such may be the man, wise in the possession of great, noble, and high-sounding ideals, whose heart is full of the sentiments of compassion ; but for all his ideals and sentiments he behaves no better than a common mortal ; he may be as petty, as easily offended, as dogged, as self-assertive as the ignorant. Like the fool, he may not know the way to the city. What profits his idealism ? His weeping sentiments ? His noble principles ? No more than the spells and incantations of the charmer, who does not apply them and is bitten by the snake.

But wisdom is a religious quality as well as a moral, and, in its religious form, it presents the same possible inefficiency. A man may declare the fear of the Lord is the beginning and end of wisdom, may assent to the truth, and may constitute it as his creed—a creed

The Charmer and the Snake

sincerely believed. But his creed—his wisdom—may be of no real advantage to him. It does not save him from being bitten by a subtle self-pride or by most aggressive and offensive conceit. His wisdom may fail to make him humble. It is not simply that there is a wide interval between creed and conduct, between the ideal and the real, but the creed seems to have no power over or relation to his conduct and no charm over his character.

We are familiar in literature with portraits like Bulstrode the banker of "Middlemarch," very evangelical and very bilious, very spiritual in thought, but very mean and worldly in actuality, or like the Rev. Mr. Chadband of "Bleak House," who prayed most fervently before food, but whose god, as the actual participation in the meal so plainly showed, was his belly. These portraits may be described as caricatures, and if they are meant to portray the evangelicalism of the end of the eighteenth century as a whole, they are caricatures with all the false emphasis of caricature, but as instances of great creed and mean conduct they are true enough. It may be said that the evangelicalism of Bulstrode and Chadband was of a very narrow and vulgar order, and that if they had only had a more gracious and broader theology they would have been distinctly more pleasing personalities. They might have been, but it is not certain, for a man may hold the divinest theology, may preach it believing its truth, may have a pride in it, but at the crucial moment, when the snake is in his path, his theology may fail him, his wisdom be conspicuous by its non-appearance, and he is bitten like any ordinary ignorant mortal.

A man may believe in the God of Jesus, of Paul, of

Pessimism and Love

Augustine and Luther, believe in Him with absolute sincerity and say, This is my God. And what may happen ? Termonde, Malines, Louvain, and their devilish destruction. His theology seems to have forsaken him ! No ; not his theology, for it is there in great evidence, but the power of it and the application of it.

I imagine that most of us can illustrate the fact of experience with which we have been dealing from our own knowledge. But we ought not, because the wisdom of the charmer fails, through not being applied, to condemn his wisdom. It is ignorant to scoff at all wisdom, the wisdom of science, of moral ideals and of religion, because sometimes it is not applied and brought into practical effect, ignorant to say, for instance, when there is some glaring inconsistency between creed and conduct, " There, that is your religion ; it is not worth much." Suppose a man had connected with his house an ingenious mode of escape in case fire should break out, and suppose his house took fire, but in some sheer stupidity he refused, or through some physical disability he was unable, in the hour of danger, to make use of the escape and suffered a scorching fate, it would be ignorance to say, "That fire-escape of his is no use ; it ought to be scrapped." Even if religion were only a fire-escape, one ought not to scoff at it, if it is not put to use and practice. The worth of religion is not to be estimated by the worthlessness of its professors. And it would be ignorant to scoff too roundly at the charmer who was bitten and call him a simple charlatan and a hypocrite. No doubt in the past he had charmed many a snake into a harmless creeping thing. It is foolish to call

The Charmer and the Snake

every man whose creed seems to break down on occasion or very often in practice an old hypocrite. There are very few conscious hypocrites. Hypocrisy is a blind thing, and most people who are regarded as arrant hypocrites are really blind to their own hypocrisy.

The real permanent lesson of this fable-proverb is the truth that wisdom by itself is not enough ; we must apply it. We need not only the power of knowledge, but also the power of application. Why is it that to the power of knowledge there is lacking at times the power of application ? For the answer I go to Paul : " If I have the gift of prophecy and know all mysteries and all knowledge, and if I have all faith so as to remove mountains, but have not love, I am nothing." Wisdom is good, but it needs love to put it into application. Casaubon was a self-centred, selfish, " white-livered " ecclesiastic. If he could only have forgotten himself in what he owed to others, to his parishioners and to his young and noble-minded wife, he would have flung those endless notes and manuscripts to the dust-heap, or if he had not done that, his research would have had a human and loving interest that would have given it a real and definite purpose and so made it of service to himself and his fellow-men. And moral wisdom—the knowledge of ideals—is not enough ; it needs love to energise the ideals. We need ideals, we are very poor, earthy creatures without them, but we need also a power that leads them into action. We need wisdom and we need love. Without love wisdom rusts, it decays, it is a dead thing. That is pre-eminently true of the wisdom that is religious belief. The belief may express the highest truth, a theology of the angels, a most enlightened creed, a

Pessimism and Love

most rational faith, but without love it is powerless, it is useless lumber. " Though I have faith so as to remove mountains, but have not love, I am nothing."

Wisdom and love, these are the necessities to save us and our fellows from the bites and wounds that poison the soul. Wisdom and love, the great requisites for life and salvation—our great requisites and our great possessions. The wise men of Israel had a very democratic conception of wisdom. She was not to them the property of philosophers or great thinkers; she was not the reward of a lifelong and painful quest; she was not a sphinx holding her secrets to her own heart in a grim unbreakable silence. She was the property of him who had ears to hear; she cries aloud, utters her truth in the street and in the market-place, declares it to youth even more than to experienced age. Wisdom, the knowledge of the good and true and of the Divine Will, her word is in every heart. We all know how near she is, how democratic, how the knowledge of the good presses upon us all. We can all say, " I know wisdom; I have the truth; I know what is good. My failure is not in knowledge, but in application. I have the wisdom, but I fail to use it and the snake bites me." But love is just as democratic as wisdom. God is Love! And in the Incarnate God how democratic Love is! It goes forth to the loveless and gives itself to them; it draws nigh to the sinful and selfish that they may lovely be. Christ is as near us all as wisdom. Christ, the love of God, is nigh us all, in our very hearts. And when that Love, with its power, comes into our life it turns our wisdom, intellectual, moral and religious, into living energies and loving activity. Whatever power, talent, knowledge,

The Charmer and the Snake

or gift we have, Love will not let it rust or decay or fail of application. Love drives the machinery of life.

There is a feeling which sometimes comes over the heart, even the heart of the most humble, a feeling that we have not made the practical most of what we have. We have received freely knowledge, wisdom, truth, but we have not freely given. Love will make the freely received the freely given. We need the Perfect Wisdom, we need no less the Perfect Love. And these are one in Christ, freely and democratically given to all.

IMPERFECT CONDITIONS

He that watcheth the wind shall not sow,
And he that is always looking at the clouds shall not reap.—CHAP. XI. 4.

For the sowing of seed by the hand a calm and windless day is an advantage ; the seed is not blown away as soon as it is cast ; and for harvest, fine weather is a necessity. The farmer should, therefore, choose his days for these respective operations ; he should observe the wind in the spring and regard the weather in the autumn. But observation of the wind will not sow his seed nor watching the weather gather in his harvest. He may watch the wind too long, waiting for an ideal day which never comes, and spring may be over before ever his seed finds the soil. Eager for a spell of perfect harvest weather, he may regard the clouds with anxious care, he may spend days in a spirit of nervous expectancy, but all the time autumn is slipping past, and, when the harvest should be stored, his corn is still standing in the field. In a word, he may be so anxious for perfect conditions that the actual thing—the sowing or the reaping—is never done. Anxiety destroys action. Of course, the farmer would act more wisely and more effectually, if he seized the first decently favourable day that the spring gave, and snatched in the autumn at any brief day of sunshine or any short interval of fine weather for his reaping and ingathering. When the business can be done at all, the wise and

Imperfect Conditions

effectual thing is to do it at once. Waiting for ideal circumstances may find the fields unsown when they should be showing promise of harvest and the barns empty when they should be full. The idealist, in this sense, will prove a poor, useless, and, probably, bankrupt farmer.

It is a parable or allegory that the wise man here utters, and, though agriculture (along with seafaring) is most immediately and directly affected by the natural conditions of wind and cloud, the warning which the parable gives is applicable to almost every occupation, trade, or business. I once knew a youth who through the kindness of a friend was successful in obtaining a post in a large engineering-works. After a short trial at the business the youth came to see his friend, who was not a little disappointed to learn that he was not very enthusiastic. The youth complained of the early start on the raw winter mornings, and that when he got to the works he felt the iron very cold. Perhaps he thought the metal should be heated to a nice temperature for his comfortable convenience or that the firm might provide muffs or hot-water bottles for the apprentices ; but whatever he may have thought regarding his own comfortable preferences, he was much more concerned with the somewhat hard but perfectly natural conditions of his occupation than with the excellence of the opportunity that had been presented to him. He was observing the wind and regarding the clouds. I know not where or what he is to-day, but I should be very much surprised to hear that he is a skilful mechanic or a great engineer. In some form or other the wind and the clouds are in every occupation. They may not be raw, wintry

Pessimism and Love

mornings and cold iron; they may be a hard and disagreeable foreman, they may be small and disproportionate remuneration, they may be the possibility of serious dangers, they will be some adverse unideal circumstances, some untoward conditions; for these exist in every calling, in merchandise, in arts and crafts, in teaching and preaching, in leadership and humble service. There never yet existed a situation over which contrary winds blew not and dark clouds hovered not, but he that spends his thought and time in anxious consideration of them will never reap much from his situation.

The temper of hesitating, of waiting, usually in vain, for perfect conditions, with its consequent querulousness, is foolish. There is nothing heroic about it; it has nothing in it that calls forth admiration; it is a real hindrance to actual accomplishment. It is not only foolish and futile, it rests upon false conceptions, arises out of totally wrong ideas. The man who expects perfectly ideal conditions for himself and his work really imagines that the world exists and is specially built for his convenience and preferences; and, though the pleasing fact may not be apparent while the contrary wind blows and the black clouds overhang, he thinks that he has only to wait and then the world will reveal its beneficent purpose and concentrate all its energies on his convenience and comfort. That is a simple delusion. One has only to think of the world with its unimaginable immensities, with its inscrutable forces all concentrated in meeting the preferences and suitable convenience of one single individual. That were indeed " a steam crane to lift a fly." The idea is absurd. Even within the limits of our own personal

Imperfect Conditions

life our own convenience is not the most important thing, and Nature and the larger life round about us are not likely to make the mistake of thinking it is. Our comfortable convenience is never the be-all and end-all of that microcosm which is the self; it is scarcely likely even for one single moment to be the be-all and end-all of the macrocosm which is Nature.

But there is another false idea on which this hesitating and semi-pessimistic temper rests, and that is the idea that this world is perfect. It is not, either in the whole or in any part. It is a world coming into being, incomplete and imperfect, with its imperfection appearing not simply in men and women, but in every condition and thing—*sunt lachrymæ rerum;* and, there is no immediate prospect of this universal imperfection vanishing with the wind or with the clouds, and the man who spends his day in waiting to see it depart will at evening have little to his account—he will neither have sowed nor reaped. In an imperfect world the counsel of wisdom is, not to wait for the perfect day that never comes, but to make the best of moderate weather, to sow while there is half a chance, to reap though clouds threaten, to grip the cold iron and for oneself to strike it into a heat; when a thing can be done at all, to do it to the utmost conditions will permit, thankful that one is allowed to make an attempt, even though perfection cannot come.

But this parable has meaning for other things besides trade, business, or occupation. A man's calling may take up the larger part of his life, but it is not his whole life, it is not meant to be. With some men, it is true, their occupation is their whole life; it absorbs their whole thought, their feeling, their every vital

Pessimism and Love

moment. They become immersed in one thing, almost to the same extent as in the earlier and middle centuries of the Christian Church, the most zealous, forsaking every other interest, retiring to the desert or making their habitation in caves, became immersed in one thing —religion, with its prayer and meditation. The Christian life was resolved into an *askesis*, into the one discipline of religious exercise, into asceticism. Now asceticism had this result. It slew many a fair and beautiful human impulse; it robbed man of many a legitimate interest; it crucified half his humanity and left him half-dead with only one poor threadbare compensation—his *askesis*.

That old *askesis* is not very common to-day, but there is a new kind—a total absorption and concentration of the whole energies on one's profession or business, but the new has the same result as the old in narrowing and impoverishing life. Man cannot live by bread alone. Commercial asceticism is robbery of life. For the full possession of life man must have more than commercial ambitions; he requires moral ideals, which, while they may guide him in his occupation, have a light and allurement of their own. He has to keep those ideals bright and burnished; he has to direct their rays upon his activities, thoughts, and feelings. In a word, for the fulness of life man has to cultivate character, to sow in the field of moral realities and to reap harvests in kind. This care for ideals gives a dignity and distinction to life; it keeps the spirit of youth with us as the years pass over us, throwing out before us as it does long stretches of country, far and ever-extending horizons, and giving us always something for which to live. With ideals,

Imperfect Conditions

there is always more of life before us than there is behind us.

But in the keeping and cultivation of ideals, in the training of our moral life, it is profoundly true that he who watches the wind shall not sow, and he who is for ever regarding the clouds shall not reap. And in the sowing and reaping of moral character there are contrary winds and dark, heavy clouds. There is one's own self, the self that approves the better but is instinctively prone to follow the worst—there is weak will and imperfect desire, and there are the clouds of uncongenial moral environment. A man looks at himself, his own imperfect heart and will, and says, " With these I cannot attain the ideal," or at his moral surroundings, and says, " Amidst these conditions I can never be perfect, can never attain to my best." The wind and the clouds of his weak self and discouraging environment make the absolutely perfect ideal impossible of realisation. And if he continues to concentrate his attention on the two obvious facts, his imperfect surroundings and his imperfect self and their hampering tendencies, he will neither sow nor reap moral character at all. He will cease to seek and to pursue the ideal. He will give up ideals as hopeless, and be content with an easy accommodation to the standards of custom and convention. He will cease to be a living moral personality. But that is not the way of wisdom. For though through wind and cloud he cannot get an absolutely perfect character, he can get some character, and that perhaps of a better quality than would have been his, if all the conditions had been favourable. Some living moral character is better than none, for that is what it amounts to when ideals

Pessimism and Love

are hopelessly abandoned. In morals it is profoundly true, " half a loaf is better than no bread." A farmer who helplessly refrained from cultivating his land, because a perfect harvest could not be always certain, would be a fool. He might get some kind of harvest, a harvest that more than paid him for his outlay of capital and labour. If simply because he cannot get glorious harvests he never sows and reaps, he will soon cease to be a farmer at all. And a man who abandons ideals because he cannot attain them to perfection is a fool. He might win some moral character, but his preoccupation with contrary winds and dark clouds which leads him to give up the quest of the ideal will rob him of moral personality, of vital and virile morality—he will cease to be a moral person in the real sense of the term. In an imperfect world, in a world where absolute moral perfection is impossible, the order of wisdom is, Sow as best you can, cultivate to the utmost which the conditions will allow. There will be some harvest at least worthy of all the outlay ; the moral ideal will be retained, and with it moral personality and the spirit of endless youth.

" The common problem, yours, mine, every one's,
Is not to fancy what were fair in life—
Providing it could be—but, finding first
What may be, then find out how to make it fair,
Up to our means—a very different thing."

There is not only the field of morality, there is also the field of religion. And in the latter it is superlatively true that he who watcheth the wind shall not sow, and he that is for ever regarding the clouds shall not reap. What is religion ? It is essentially, though not com-

Imperfect Conditions

pletely, defined as the knowledge of God and a living in communion with Him. But what do we mean by God? When Simonides was asked that question he demanded first a day to think about the answer, then two days more, and, after that, continuously doubled the required time when the time already granted had come to an end, but without ever finding that he was able to produce the required answer: rather more apt to suspect that the answer carried him beyond the range of human intelligence. Truly, no man by searching can find out God. No man can find God completely and to perfection in His infinite, universal, and eternal being. But because man cannot find out God to completion and to perfection, shall he on that account refuse to know God at all?—refuse to commune with Him as He has been revealed to human conscience and heart, in history, in nature, in grace, in the face of Jesus Christ? Because a perfect and complete knowledge of God is impossible, shall man hesitate and wait until the books be opened and the eternities be completely revealed and his own eyes so gifted with supernatural vision that he can behold them and read them from eternal beginning to eternal end? Shall he because God dwelleth for ever in mystery refuse to know Him as love, as forgiveness, as a kindly Father and gracious Providence—a knowledge which illumines life and gives hope, strength, and joy to the heart? Shall man refuse to enjoy the genial rays of light because he cannot know the composition of that Perfect Sun which is the Infinite and Eternal God? To do so is to watch the wind and regard the clouds, with the result that there will be no sowing or reaping in the field of religion. Or shall a man give up religion

Pessimism and Love

because someone writes a sceptical article, questioning a miracle or the miraculous as a whole, or the logical consistency of some doctrine, and hold aloof from a faith which has proved itself, even in its imperfect intellectual forms, as a strength to overcome and as an instrument of joyous and courageous living ? Or shall one stand apart from the Church of Christ because some hypocrisy appears in it, some pride and vanity, some stain and sin ? Shall one, because the Church is not perfect, wait till it is, before one gives it the light of his countenance, the honour of his approval, and the help of his patronage—shall one go on in querulous hesitation and critical aloofness and not rather snatch the opportunity which even an imperfect Church gives of realising social religion and its virtues of charity, mutual forbearance, and common helpfulness ? The man who is waiting till personal religion is a perfect communion or till theology has become the complete and final form of truth, and organised religion is fair and beautiful as a spotless sun, will lose the light, the joy, the strength, the realities of religion altogether. His life at its very sources will be dried up.

We live in an imperfect world. Continuous preoccupation with its imperfections is futile—futile in ordinary occupations, in our moral cultivation, and not least in religion. We cannot even imagine a perfect world; but let us suppose a world in which every man, working under perfect conditions, perfectly fulfilled his calling of craftsman or teacher or man of business, that also every man under perfect conditions could realise perfectly the moral ideal and could know God perfectly face to face. What more would there be to live for ? We should have obtained the absolute perfection in

Imperfect Conditions

this world, we should have no looking forward. We should have got to the end of things—an end of things very like death, for we live by hope.

Such a world does not seem so good as one with contrary winds and threatening clouds, which calls for courage and energy, that will, in spite of imperfect conditions, win a fair and good harvest. The imperfections of the world are not for observation, but for overcoming, so that a man may have something of a victory that he can call his own.

LOVE SONGS OF THE BIBLE

NUPTIAL SONGS

Translations and Brief Notes

The so-called "Song of Songs" is a beautiful collection of nuptial ballads, a garland of verse with one theme, the love of man and woman. During the honeymoon, which lasted seven days, the bridegroom, though he was but a poor peasant, reigned as a king and the bride as a queen; indeed, he, for that one week, became glorious as Solomon and she was accounted as beautiful as Abishag the Shunammite (cf. 1 Kings i. 2). The threshing sledge was brought out, decorated, and raised on a scaffold, and became a very throne where bride and bridegroom sat in their glory. Everybody and everything was idealised and surrounded with the pomp and circumstance of royalty: the friends of the bridegroom are "the choice warriors of Solomon," the humble home of the bride is a "cedar palace," and her friends are "the daughters of Jerusalem." The peasant and his bride were given a royal week.

These songs are full of the loveliness of Nature. They carry us into the open air, to the vineyards, the villages and mountains; they exhale the scent of the forest trees, of apples and pomegranates; we see, as we read them, fields embroidered with lilies, the swift and timid gazelles, and hear the sound of the birds. Nature in all her richness is in the songs. They are also rich with all the pomp and circumstance of a royal court and a royal procession; they find delight in the rich attire of women, their jewels and perfumes. No doubt in parts the lusciousness of the imagery and the detailed descriptions of physical charms offend our modern taste. But these poems are not modern (in form at least), but go back beyond the Christian centuries; nor were they written for civilised Western peoples, but for Orientals, to whom *naturalia non sunt turpia*. But we may forgive what seems to us in these poems indelicate or even indecent for that glorious description of love in CHAP. VIII. 6, 7, which can take its place with the best in the world's poetry of human love.

The question of authorship is an idle one. Folk songs do not have authors. They are fortunate when they find an editor.

As for the date of these songs, the language points to a late period, probably the second century B.C. or later.

I. SONG OF THE BRIDE

Let him kiss me with kisses of his mouth;
For better are thy caresses than wine.
Pleasant and fragrant are thine ointments,[1]
An ointment poured forth is thy name;[2]
Therefore do the maidens love thee.
Draw me after thee; let us hasten.

---

[1] Ointments were abundantly used by the Easterns on account of their fragrance, and were a sign of joy.
[2] "Thy name." Name is equivalent to the person. Or perhaps the idea is that the very mention of the Bridegroom's name creates a fragrance.

Love Songs of the Bible

The king hath brought me to his chamber !
We will exult and we will rejoice in thee,
We will celebrate thy caresses above wine.
    Right is one in loving thee.—CHAP. I. 2—4.

II. SONGS OF THE BRIDE AND THE BRIDEGROOM
THE BRIDE

Sunburnt, yet fair am I, O daughters of Jerusalem,
Dark like the swarthy tints of Kedar, yet beautiful as the hangings of Solomon.
Take no regard to my swarthiness,
For it is the sun that hath streamed upon me.
The sons of my mother were angry with me,
And they set me as keeper of the vineyards ;[1]
Yet mine own vineyard have I not kept.

Tell me, thou whom my soul loveth,[2]
Where thou shepherdst thy sheep,
Where thou dost repose them at noontide.

---

[1] The brothers of the Bride were angry with her on some occasion or other, and sent her to watch the vineyards. But her own vineyard, that is, the love of her heart, she did not guard. While watching the vineyards she gave her love away. The anger of the brothers was a blessing in disguise.

[2] The connection here is difficult. The question and answer may best be regarded as an independent fragment of a song. Nor is it stated who it is that gives the answer. It may be the Bride's companions, or it might come quite naturally out of her own knowledge. The bride knew before she put the question where she was likely to find her beloved at noonday.

Pessimism and Love

Why should I be like a wandering woman
By the flocks of thy companions?
"If thou dost not know for thyself, thou fairest of women,
Get thee hence to the trails of the flock
And pasture thy goats by the tents of the shepherds."

THE BRIDEGROOM

To a filly yoked to the chariot of Pharaoh do I liken thee, my friend.[1]
Lovely are thy cheeks with plaits,
Thy neck with strings of beads.
Plaits of gold will we make for thee
With points of silver.

THE BRIDE

While the king was on his festal tour
My nard gave forth its fragrance.
Like the bag of myrrh, which reposes between my breasts, is my beloved to me;
Like a cluster of henna, which grows in the vineyards of Engedi, is my beloved to me.

THE BRIDEGROOM

Behold thou art beautiful, my friend;
Behold thou art beautiful; doves' eyes are thine eyes.

[1] This is the answer of the Bridegroom to the Bride's disparagement of her sunburnt beauty.

Love Songs of the Bible

THE BRIDE
Behold thou art beautiful, my love, yea a delight;
Yea our couch is luxuriant.
The beams of our house are cedars,
And our rafters are cypress.
I am a meadow-saffron of the Sharon-plain :
A lily of the valleys.

THE BRIDEGROOM
As a lily among the thorns,
So is my friend among the young women.

THE BRIDE
As an apple tree amongst the trees of the forest,
So is my beloved among the young men.
I delighted to sit down beneath his shadow,
And his fruit was sweet to my taste.
He has brought me to the house of wine,
And his banner over me is love.
Sustain me with cakes of raisins.[1]
Strengthen me with apples ;
For weak with love am I.
His left arm is under my head,
And his right embraces me.
I adjure you, O daughters of Jerusalem,
By the gazelles or the hinds of the field,
That ye stir not up, that ye rouse not love,
Until it please.—CHAP. I. 5, II. 7.

---

[1] Cakes of raisins and apples may be figuratively used for kisses and caresses.

Pessimism and Love

III. SONG OF THE BRIDE

Hark ! my beloved ! see there he comes !
Leaping over the mountains, skipping over the hills.
Like a gazelle is my beloved, or like a young stag.
See, there he is, standing behind our house wall,
Spying in through the windows,
Glancing through the lattices.
My beloved speaks and says to me,
" Rise, rise, my friend, my beauty, come, come ;
For lo ! the winter is past, the rain is over, it is clean away.
The flowers appear in the country ;
The time for pruning is at hand,
And the song of the turtle dove is heard.
And the fig tree is fruiting its first green figs,
And the vines are all blossom and give forth perfume."
I seized him and would not let slack my hold of him
Until I brought him to the house of my mother,
And unto the chamber of her who bare me.
I adjure you, O daughters of Jerusalem,
By the gazelles or by the hinds of the field,
That ye stir not up, that ye rouse not love,
Until it please.—CHAPS. II. 8—13*a*, III. 4*b*—5.

Love Songs of the Bible

IV. SONG OF THE BRIDE (in which she recounts a dream, reminiscent of the pre-nuptial time)

Upon my bed at nights I sought him whom my soul loveth;
   I sought him and found him not.
" I will arise," I said, "and go round the city;
In the streets and broad places will I seek him whom my soul loveth."
   I sought him and found him not.
The watchmen that go their rounds in the city, they found me.
" Have ye seen," asked I, " him whom my soul loveth?"
   But a little had I passed from them,
When I found him whom my soul loveth.

" Rise, rise, my friend, my beauty; come, come away,
My dove who art in the secret clefts of the crag, in the shadow of the steep.
Let me see thy form, let me hear thy voice,
   For thy voice is sweet and thy form delightful."

[Lay hold for us of the foxes, the small foxes that spoil our vineyards,
While our vineyards are in blossom.[1]]

---

[1] Lay hold of the young foxes, etc. This couplet is probably an interpolation. It is an appeal for the chivalrous protection of maidenhood.

Pessimism and Love

My beloved is mine and I am his,
 Who shepherdeth by the lilies
Until the day blow cool and the shadows flee away.
Become like the gazelle, my beloved, like a young stag,
On the mountains of the sweet-smelling Malabathron.[1]—CHAPS. III. 1—4a, II. 13b—17.

SONG V. (Description of the Bridegroom on his nuptial tour)
What is this, then, coming up out of the wilderness like columns of smoke,
Scented with myrrh and frankincense, with all the powders of the merchant?
See! it is the litter of Solomon,[2]
With sixty of the chivalry round about it,
 Of the chivalry of Israel,
All of them girt with the sword, skilled warriors,
Each with his sword upon his thigh,
A defence against the terror in the night-seasons.
A sedan hath the king Solomon had made for himself,
 Out of the wood of Lebanon.

[1] Malabathron, an aromatic spice. The meaning is figurative. The Bride had placed a packet of myrrh on her bosom. See CHAP. I. 13.
[2] The litter of Solomon is the royal car with which the threshing waggon is poetically compared. The Bridegroom, with a diadem on his head, is seated on the threshing waggon gloriously decorated and made, for the time, like a royal equipage.

Love Songs of the Bible

The pillars thereof he had them made of silver,
  The supports thereof of gold,
  The seat thereof of purple,
  The interior thereof is fitted out with ebony.[1]
Go forth, ye daughters of Zion, and look on King Solomon,
At the crown with which his mother crowned him in the day of his espousals,
Yea, in the day of the joy of his heart.
  CHAP. III. 6—11.

SONG VI. (Sung in praise of the beauty of the Bride)

Lo! thou art beautiful, my friend; thou art beautiful.
Thine eyes are like doves' eyes,
Glancing from behind thy veil;
Thy hair is like the flock of goats
Which hang on the slopes of Mount Gilead.
Thy teeth are like a flock of ewes new-shorn,[2]
Which come up from the washing,
Which all cast twins,[3]
And there is not one barren among them.

---

[1] Fitted out with ebony. This translation is obtained by a slight but necessary emendation of the Hebrew text.

[2] Compare Burns:—"On Cessnock Banks"
  " Her teeth are like a flock of sheep
  With fleeces newly washen clean,
  That slowly mount the rising steep;
    And she's twa glancin' sparklin' een."

[3] Frequently in Hebrew poetry the comparison, as here, is carried on to points which are not directly relevant.

Pessimism and Love

As a scarlet thread are thy lips,
And thy mouth is charming;
As a cleft of pomegranate is thy temple
Behind thy veil.
As the tower of David is thy neck,
Whereon hang a thousand shields,
All of them the weapons of heroes.
Thy two breasts are like two stag twins of a gazelle,
Which feed among the lilies,
Until the day blow cool, and the shadows flee away.
As for me, I will go unto the mount of myrrh,
And unto the hill of frankincense.
Beautiful every whit art thou, my friend,
There is no fault in thee.

. . . . . [1]

Thou hast ravished me, my sister and bride;
Thou hast ravished me through one glance of thine eyes,
Through one gleam from the pendant of thy necklace.
How lovely are thy caresses, my sister and bride!
How sweet are thy caresses, sweeter than wine!

---

[1] Here Chap. IV. 7 appear five lines which seem out of place—
"With me from Lebanon, my bride,
With me from Lebanon come:
Go from the top of Amana,
From the top of Senir and Hermon,
Away from the lions' dens,
From the mountains of the leopards."

Love Songs of the Bible

And the perfume of thine ointments than all
 spices !
From thy lips doth drop virgin honey, O bride :
Honey and milk are beneath thy tongue ;
And the smell of thy garments is as the smell of
 Lebanon.
A garden barred is my sister and bride ;
A garden barred, a well sealed is she.
Thy shoots are a park of pomegranates with
 choicest fruits ;
Henna with plants of nard,
Nard and saffron, the reed and cinnamon,
With trees of all kinds of frankincense ;
Myrrh and aloes, with all the chief spices.
The fountain of my garden [1] is a spring of living
 waters ;
Yea of flowing streams from Lebanon.

The Bride, keeping to the figure of the garden, expresses the desire that her charms may attract the Bridegroom to herself.

Awake, O north wind ; and come, O south ;
Let my garden send forth perfumes.
Let the spices flow therefrom.
Let my beloved come to his garden ;
Let him eat his choicest fruits.

---

[1] By a slight change of the Hebrew text.

Pessimism and Love

The Bridegroom closes the song with a description of his delight in love fulfilled and an appeal to his friends to enjoy the same delight.

I enter my garden, my sister and bride :
I gather my myrrh with my balsam ;
I eat my honeycomb with my honey ;
I drink my wine like milk :
Eat, comrades ;
Drink, drink lustily, my friends.
CHAPS. IV. 1—V. 1.

SONG VII. (In praise of the Bridegroom and put into the mouth of the Bride)
I was sleeping, yet my heart was awake.
Hark ! my beloved is knocking.

THE BRIDEGROOM
" Open for me, my sister, my friend, my love, my perfect one ;
For my head is covered with dew, my locks with drops of the night."

THE BRIDE
" I have removed my tunic ;
Why should I put it on again ?
I have washed my feet ;
Why should I soil them again ? "
My beloved stretched forth his hand through the lattice,

Love Songs of the Bible

And my passion thrilled with desire for him.
I rose to open for my beloved ;
My hands dropped myrrh,
And my fingers flowing-myrrh,
Flowing and dropping on the catches of the bolt.
I opened for my beloved ;
And my beloved had turned away, vanished.
My heart went out of me when he vanished.[1]
I sought him and found him not ;
I called him, and he answered me not.
The watchmen found me that go their rounds in the city.
They smote me, they bruised me ;
They lifted my wrap from me, the watchers of the walls.
I adjure you, ye daughters of Jerusalem,
If ye find my beloved—what will ye say to him ?
Say, sick with love am I.

" How is thy beloved better than another, thou fairest among women?
What is thy beloved better than another,
That thou shouldest so adjure us ? "[2]

My beloved is dazzling and ruddy,
Distinguished among ten thousand.
His head is fine gold,

[1] When he vanished. This is obtained by a slight change in the Hebrew text.
[2] Spoken by the friends of the Bride, as we should say "the bridesmaids," who, in the following lines, are answered by the Bride.

Pessimism and Love

His locks are waving,
Black as the raven.
His eyes are like those of doves,
That are beside the water-brooks,
They bathe themselves in milk.
His cheeks are like terraces of balsam
That emit rich perfumes.
His hands are cylinders of gold set with yellow jasper.
His body is shining ivory
Covered with sapphires.
His legs are pillars of marble
Set upon sockets of fine gold.
His whole aspect is like Lebanon,
Choice like the cedars.
His mouth is sweetness itself :
His whole being is greatly to be desired.
This is my beloved, and this is my friend,
O daughters of Jerusalem.

" Where hath thy beloved gone,
Thou fairest among women ?
Where hath thy beloved turned,
That we may seek him with thee ? "
My beloved hath gone down to his garden,[1]
To the terraces of balsam,
To pasture in the gardens,

---

[1] To his garden ; that is, to his Bride and his delight in her charms.

Love Songs of the Bible

And to glean the lilies.
I am my beloved's, and my beloved is mine ;
He that pastureth among the lilies.

CHAPS. V. 2—VI. 3.

SONG VIII. (In praise of the Bride, put into the mouth of the Bridegroom)

Beautiful art thou, my friend, as Tirzah,
Lovely as Jerusalem,
Yet awe-inspiring as hosts called to the flag.
Turn thine eyes from me, for they raise a storm within me.
Thy hair is like a flock of goats that hang upon the slopes of Gilead.
Thy teeth are like a flock of ewes that go up from the washing :
All of them cast twins ;
And there is not a barren one amongst them.
As a cleft of pomegranate is thy temple
Behind thy veil.
Sixty wives and eighty concubines had Solomon,
And young women without number,
But The One is my Dove, my perfect one ;
The only one is she of her mother,
The choice one of her who bare her.
The daughters saw her and counted her happy,
The queens and concubines also, and sang her praise.

Pessimism and Love

[Who is this that looketh like the slanting rays
    of the morning,
Fair as the moon,
Clear as the sun,
Awe-inspiring like hosts called to the flag ? [1]]
I have gone down into the garden of nuts
To see the green shoots in the wady,
To see if the vine be sprouting,
And if the pomegranates be in flower.

CHAP. VI. 4—11.

. . . . . .[2]

SONG IX. (In praise of the Bride, who engages
    in a sword dance, which was evidently part
    of the nuptial entertainment)
Who is this that looketh like the slanting rays of
    the morning :
Fair as the moon,
Clear as the sun,
Yet awe-inspiring as hosts called to the flag ? [3]

---

[1] This verse is out of place here. It makes a fitting beginning of the next song.

[2] Chap. VI. 12 in A.V. is very difficult. A sure meaning is impossible to obtain. Taking the words as they stand, we might translate,
    " Or ever I knew, my soul set me
        In the chariots of my generous people."
But the meaning and connection are very obscure. The text has probably suffered both corruption and misplacement.

[3] Amongst Oriental tribes it was the custom, at the celebration of a victory, for a woman to dance the sword dance. If a young man became enamoured of her beauty, he might make the attempt to draw near to her ; she, on her part, could ward him off with the sword. In this attempt he might be wounded or even killed, for according to the rules of the game he was allowed only to use the left arm. The Shulammite is compared with one of these terrible Amazons.

Love Songs of the Bible

Turn thee, turn thee, O Shulammite,[1]
Turn thyself around.
What do ye see in the Shulammite?
We see dancing like the dancing of two armies.
How beautiful are thy steps in sandals, O daughter of a Prince!
The curves of thy thighs are like ornaments,
Craft of an artist's hand.
Seductive art thou like a rounded bowl;
May the wine of love never fail thee.
Thy belly is a heap of wheat
Enclosed with lilies;
Thy two breasts are like the two twin stags of a gazelle;
Thy neck is like a tower of ivory;
Thine eyes are like pools in Heshbon,
At the gate of Bath-rabbim;
Thy nose is like the tower of Lebanon
That looketh toward Damascus.
Thy head upon thee is as Carmel,
And thy flowing locks like purple;
In the tresses thereof is the king bound.
How beautiful, how lovely, art thou, O my love, in the delights of love.
This, thy stature, is like to a palm tree,

---

[1] Shulammite. Daughter of Shulem, or Shunem (see 1 Kings i. 3). The peasant is compared with Abishag for beauty, in fact is a second Abishag. Shulammite means really "Thou most beautiful among women."

Pessimism and Love

And thy breasts like clusters.
I said, " I will go up the palm tree,
I will lay fast hold of the branches,
And thy breasts shall be to me as clusters of the
    vine,
And the perfume of thy nose as that from apples ;
And thy mouth shall be as the best wine,
Gliding over the lips and teeth."[1]
                    CHAPS. VI. 10—VII. 1—9.

SONG X. (Put into the mouth of the Bride)
I am my beloved's,
And his desire is toward me.
Come, my beloved, let us go forth to the field ;
Let us lodge among the henna-flowers ;
Let us rise and go early to the vineyards ;
Let us see if the vine hath sprouted,
And the blossom hath opened,
And if the pomegranates be in flower ;
There will I give my caresses to thee :
The love apples give forth their scent,
And over our doors are all choice fruits,
Yea, new and old,
My beloved ; I have stored them for thee.
Oh ! that thou wert my brother,
That sucked at the breasts of my mother,

---

[1] Translating from the LXX.

Love Songs of the Bible

Then, should I find thee in the street, I would kiss thee,
Yea, and the folk would not despise me.
Let me lead thee, let me bring thee to the house of my mother,
Into the chamber of her that conceived me : [1]
I would give thee to drink of the spiced wine,
Of the pressed juice of the pomegranate.
His left hand lies under my head,
And his right doth embrace me.
I adjure you, ye daughters of Jerusalem,
That ye stir not up, arouse not love,
Until it please.—CHAPS. VII. 10—13—VIII. 1—4.

XI. FRAGMENTS OF SONGS

(a) Who is this that cometh from the plain,
Leaning herself on her beloved ?
CHAP. VIII. 5a.

(b) Under the apple tree have I thee awakened :
There lay in travail thy mother with thee :
There lay in travail she who bare thee.
CHAP. VIII. 5b.

(c) Set me as a seal upon thine heart,[2]
As a seal upon thine arm :

---

[1] Adopting the reading of the LXX.
[2] This fragment (c) is the most beautiful song of the book. It is a noble piece of literature, and should find its place in every anthology of love poetry.

Pessimism and Love

For strong as death is love ;
Inexorable as Sheol[1] is passion ;
Its flames are flames of fire,
The very flame of Yah.[2]
Many waters cannot quench this love.
Neither can streams in spate sweep it away.
If a man would give all the substance of his house for love,
Despised, despised let him be.

CHAP. VIII, 6, 7.

(d) We have a little sister,[3]
And she hath no breasts :
What shall we do with our sister,
In the day when she shall be spoken for ?
If she be a wall,
We will build about her a battlement of silver ;
But if she be an open door,
We will enclose her with boards of cedar.

The Bride answers the brothers.

I am a wall,
And my breasts are like towers ;

---

[1] Sheol—the place of the dead, here practically equivalent to Death itself.
[2] Yah = Jehovah, the Almighty.
[3] The brothers have a young sister. If she be modest, they will expect from her bridegroom a good dowry at the day when she is marriageable. If she be immodest, they will protect her against herself. The Bride is modest and has come to her full womanhood and finds her joy in giving herself to her husband.

Love Songs of the Bible

Then was I in his eyes as one that found
    peace.—Chap. VIII. 8—10.

(e) Solomon had a vineyard in Baal-Hamon : [1]
He gave the vineyard out to keepers ;
Each one brought for the fruit thereof
A thousand shekels of silver.
My vineyard,[2] which is mine, is before me :
The thousand shekels be thine, O Solomon,
And two hundred shekels to those that keep
    the fruit thereof.—Chap. VIII. 11, 12.

(f) Denizen of the gardens!
Companions hearken to thy voice.
Let me hear it.—Chap. VIII. 13.

(g) Flee, my beloved!
And be thou like a gazelle or a young stag
Upon the mountains of spices.
                  Chap. VIII. 14.

---

[1] This fragment (e) is from the Bridegroom. His one and perfect Bride is more to him than all the wealth of Solomon.

[2] "My Vineyard"—i.e., My Bride.

BIBLIOGRAPHY

The following bibliography is very far from complete. Only English work has been mentioned. The books in italics are specially suitable for the general reader, to whom this brief bibliography may prove helpful.

I.—ECCLESIASTES

BIBLE DICTIONARIES

Hastings' " Bible Dictionary." Articles, " Wisdom " and " Ecclesiastes."

Cheyne's " Encyclopædia Biblica." Article, " Ecclesiastes."

INTRODUCTIONS

S. R. Driver. " Introduction to the Literature of the Old Testament."

G. B. Gray. *" A Critical Introduction to the Old Testament."*

J. E. McFadyen. *" An Introduction to the Old Testament."* (Indicates clearly the composite nature of Ecclesiastes.)

Bennett and Adeney. " A Biblical Introduction."

A. H. McNeile. " An Introduction to the Book of Ecclesiastes."

COMMENTARIES

G. A. Barton. " International Critical."

C. H. H. Wright. " The Book of Koheleth."

G. C. Martin. " Century Bible " : *Proverbs, Ecclesiastes, and Song of Solomon.*

E. H. Plumptre. " Cambridge Bible." (Rich in literary illustration.)

> NOTE.—None of the above Commentaries (except *"International Critical,"* which allows for small contributions from two later editors) is written on the basis of the composite character of Ecclesiastes.

GENERAL

S. Cox. " The Expositor's Bible."

G. G. Bradley. " Lectures on Ecclesiastes."

T. K. Cheyne. " Job and Solomon."

W. T. Davison. " The Wisdom Literature of the Old Testament."

Bibliography

J. F. Genung. " *The Hebrew Literature of Wisdom in the Light of To-day.*"

E. J. Dillon. " The Sceptics of the Old Testament."

W. Harvey-Jellie. " The Wisdom of God and the Word of God."

II.—SONG OF SONGS

Dictionaries and Introductions the same as for Ecclesiastes.

COMMENTARIES

W. F. Adeney. " *Expositor's Bible.*" (Written on the dramatic theory for which Biblical introductions should be consulted.)

G. C. Martin. " *Century Bible* " : *Proverbs, Ecclesiastes, and Song of Solomon.*

A. Harper. " *Cambridge Bible.*"

W. W. Cannon. " The Song of Songs."

INDEX

ABISHAG the Shunammite, 235, 251 (note)
Adversity, uses of, 85 ff.
Ambition, 78 ff.
Asceticism, 226
Askesis, 226

BACON, FRANCIS, 177 f.
Beast, a creature of time and space, 57 ff.
Benson, A. C., 164
Black Watch, the, 199
"Bulstrode," 217

CALVINISM, 156
"Casaubon, Rev. Edward," 166, 213, 219
"Chadband, Rev. Mr.," 217
Christ revolutionises all values, 26 f., 36
Christ (Jesus), 91
    on immortality, 65
    on the neutrality of God, 105, 181
Coleridge, 167
Comte, 33 f.
Conscience, training of, 209 f.
    universal, 207

DICKENS ("Bleak House"), 217
Dogs, 62

ECCLESIASTES, meaning of word, 11
Eliot, George ("Middlemarch"), 166, 213, 217, 219
Epicureanism, 128 ff.
    its defects, 132 ff.
    its place in the Bible, 134
    its various forms, 129
Epicurus, 128 ff.

FAIRBAIRN, 73 (note), 89 (note)
Fatalism, 53
Faust, 39
Fiske, John, his belief in immortality, 35

GOETHE, 39
Gratitude, 156
    an avenue to God, 157

HALLAM, ARTHUR, 186, 190
Haroun Alraschid, 29
Hedonist, the, 125 ff.
Heraclitus, 179

IMMORTALITY a probability and more than a probability, 64 f.
Intelligence, cultivation of, 204 ff.
Intervention (miraculous), 108

JUBAL, legend of, 88

KOHELETH,
    his attitude to womanhood, etc., 94
    his egotism, 47
    his faith and age, 24
    his materialism, 57 ff.
    his place in the Bible, 25
    suggested translations, 11
    his wealth, 41

LIFE,
    a gift, 151 ff.
    a vocation, 204 ff.
Lockyer, Frederick, 74 (note)
Logic, 102
Love, as necessary as wisdom, 219 f.
    democratic, 220
Luck, 184 ff.
    not a blind chance, 192

Index

MAN a son of God, 63
"Middlemarch," 166, 213, 217, 219
Money, 19 f.
    the Pessimist on, 76 ff.

NATURE,
    a beneficent power, 106
    its repeating cycles, 22 f.
Neutrality, the Divine, 101 ff.
New Testament,
    conception of womanhood, 97 f.
    condemns gloominess, 86

PARROTS, 61
Pater, Walter, 87 (note), 128
Paul, St., 217, 219
Pessimism,
    bedrock, 67 ff.
    in the Bible, 69
    practical atheism, 71
Pietist, the,
    a Calvinist, 145
    criticism of, 147 ff.
    defender of orthodoxy, 143 f.
    his mental attitude, 146 f.
Programme, the Divine, does not destroy human freedom, 55

RENAN, ERNEST, 130
Reputation brief and precarious, 21
Reynolds, Sir Joshua, 100

Risk, its part in human affairs, 200 f.
    universal in life, 196
Romney, 100

SEA-LIONS, 61
Sheol, 254 (note)
Shepherd of Hermas, 86 f., 130
Solomon, 215, 235, 237, 242
Soul, cultivation of, 210
    universal, 210
Stevenson, Robert Louis, 62, 185, 189
Suffering, its necessity for joy, 92

TENNYSON,
    "The Two Voices," 12
    "The Palace of Art," 43, 48
Timeliness, 50

WIDOW's mite, 74
Wisdom,
    Biblical idea of, 165 f.
    its utility, 166
    democratic, 167
    the experiment with, 28 ff.
    has no final interpretation of life, 32
Wise man, the, 163 ff.
    a type called "the humanists of Israel," 163
Woman,
    in the N. T., 97 f.
    in the O. T., 96 f.
    more religious than man, 96
    the modern problem of, 99

www.ingramcontent.com/pod-product-compliance
Lightning Source LLC
Chambersburg PA
CBHW062012220426
43662CB00010B/1296